A BRIEF HISTORY OF THE ORKNEYS

J N Sinclair

MINERVA PRESS

LONDON
MIAMI   DELHI   SYDNEY

A BRIEF HISTORY OF THE ORKNEYS
Copyright © J N Sinclair 2000

ISBN 0 75410 949 6

First Published 2000 by
MINERVA PRESS
315–317 Regent Street
London W1R 7YB

Printed in Great Britain for Minerva Press

A BRIEF HISTORY
OF THE ORKNEYS

*I dedicate this book in memory
of my Orcadian parents*

Foreword

When one sees a grass-covered mound, a layman like myself wonders if there is anything inside it, while a solitary upright stone standing in a field makes one wonder whether it is a standing stone from a far distant prehistory period, or a stone erected in later times for a less mystical purpose. While investigating Orkney's past, I have collected information which I thought might be of interest to someone else, especially as many of the books on the subject are now out of print.

Contents

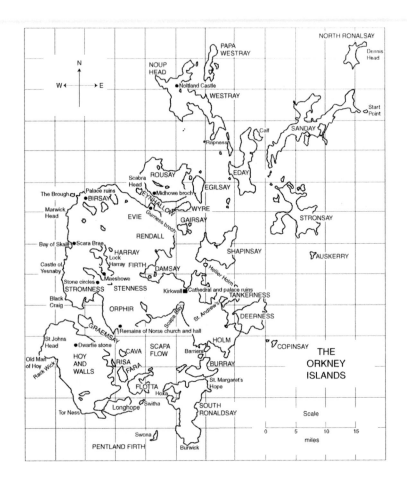

There is a group of islands
Likely north of where you be,
Which are battered by wind and waves
Common to this northern sea.

They have been called the Orkneys
Since history first began.
But maybe they should be known
As islands of the storm.

The orca could have hunted there,
That is a type of whale.
Maybe it is from it
The islands got their name.

Introduction

The Orkney Islands are situated off the north-east corner of Scotland and, although they now have an air of quiet and tranquillity, they have had their moments. In *The Lay of the Last Minstrel*, Walter Scott describes them as the 'storm swept Orcades', which is an apt description, as they lie in the path of depressions that bring strong westerly winds to the islands. It was Ptolemy, an early Egyptian, who called them the Orcades and a promontory on the northern coast of Scotland, Orcas Promontorium. Maybe the islands and the promontory got their names from a whale, the Delphinus Orca, which in the past hunted in great numbers in the sea around the Orkney Islands.

The surface rock of the islands is mainly sedimentary old red sandstone, which was deposited on top of older rock, while under the sea. Outcrops of this older rock, in the form of granite and schist, come to the surface on the island of Graemsay, on the main island at Brinkie's Brae near Stromness, and at Yesnaby. Recently this stratum of rock was found to contain some radioactive substance which caused some concern among the local residents, as did the suspicion that nuclear waste was to be dumped in the sea west of Orkney. Over the centuries the west coasts of the islands have been battered by waves from the Atlantic, which have gradually eaten away the land to produce high cliffs. At Yesnaby the cliff tops jut out over the sea, through the action of the waves combined with some difference in the structure of the cliffs there. A collapse of overhanging cliffs occurred there recently.

Thousands of years ago this part of Europe was covered by ice. About ten thousand years ago these Arctic ice fields receded northwards, and botanists inform us that when this happened, trees such as birch, elder, hazel and mountain ash flourished in Orkney. This warmer period was followed by a wet and windy period when the trees decayed.

According to Jo Ben, an early visitor to Orkney, Deerness, the parish at the extreme east of the main island, was once wooded and inhabited by deer. This is supported by the fact that tree roots and deer horns have been found buried deep in the peat moss. Probably in about the third millennium BC the wet and windy period was replaced by another warm period, during which Stone Age man arrived in Orkney.

The Stone Age village of Skara Brae, which is situated near the Bay of Skaill, was discovered in 1850, after having been buried and preserved for centuries in sand dunes. The Bay of Skaill must have had a reputation for being a very sandy bay because Sandwick, the parish it is situated in, seems to have got its name from this sandy bay, or wick. The prevailing westerly winds were continually blowing sand inland from the sand dunes at the shore of the bay, some even reaching the top of Kierfiold, a nearby hill, probably the part named Sand Field on the map. This movement of sand at the Bay of Skaill will explain why Skara Brae was buried in the sand dunes.

The stone circles are considered as belonging to the Bronze Age which followed the Stone Age and which started during the early part of the first millennium BC. The brochs were built during the Iron Age, which began towards the end of the first millennium BC, and after the broch builders Picts and Celtic monks had settled on the islands. Sculptured stones belonging to this or the early Scandinavian period which followed, have been found in northern Scotland and islands. These stones are engraved or embossed with various designs, some having the Celtic cross included. On the edges of some of these stones there are ogam inscriptions, writings in an ancient Irish alphabet.

The Scandinavians who followed the Picts didn't leave much archaeological evidence, but we know more about them through the sagas. These are narratives of this early period in the north, written down by writers who would have made full use of the verses or lays, composed by scalds, the Scandinavian equivalent of minstrels. The scald has first-hand knowledge of historical events for he accompanied his master into battle.

The main source of information concerning the Norse earls of Orkney is the *Orkneyinga Saga*, the saga of the Orkney men. It is not known who wrote this saga, but its early chapters are included in the *Olaf Saga*, written by the Icelandic saga writer Snorri Sturluson, so the *Orkneyinga Saga* must have been written some time before AD 1241, when Snorri Sturluson died.

After the Scandinavian period, documents and histories supply information and then material written in later times.

The Early Inhabitants

The first people to settle in Orkney belonged to the Neolithic period and probably came in stages from the Mediterranean. One of the reasons suggested for this is that the Scottish mainland was then covered by forests, and as the climate was then much milder, it wouldn't have been unusual to travel to the far north. They buried their dead in chamber tombs, which were built with huge stones, hence their name-tag megalithic, or 'big-stone' people.

The burial chambers of the Orkneys are usually found underneath a cairn of stones, or stones and earth, and all are entered by a low passageway. In some the remains of the dead were placed in small cells positioned in the walls of the chamber, while in others the remains were placed on the ground, separated from each other by stone partitions which give the compartments the appearance of stalls in a byre or stable. This type is known as a stalled burial chamber, of which the long burial chamber at Midhowe on the island of Rousay is the best example. At Unston in Stenness there is a stalled chamber with a burial cell in one of its walls; a combination of both types.

Also at Stenness, which is on the main island, so is easy to get to, is the Maeshowe tomb. This tomb was built about the same time as the Pyramids of Egypt, and because of its size and construction must have been a burial place of some importance. Its long, low passage and the fifteen feet square chamber are built with large stone slabs. One enters the mound through the passage. In three of the walls of the chamber, about three feet above ground level, is a burial cell and on the ground lie three wedge-shaped stone blocks, probably originally used to seal up the cells. Maeshowe was broken into during the twelfth century by Norsemen who were waiting to go to the Holy Land with Earl Rognvald, and they cut runic inscriptions and the likeness of a dragon into the stone. One of the inscriptions tells how 'Jerusalem-farers' opened the mound, while another describes how the treasure was carried away. These runes are modified characters from the Roman and Greek alphabets, which were altered to make it easier to cut them into wood or stone. Old photos show a hole in the roof of the chamber where the mound was entered, although this has now been sealed with covering.

On the island of Hoy, in a lonely valley between Ward Hill and the Knap of Trowieglen, is an ancient monument known as the Dwarfie Stone. This sandstone block has evidently fallen from the Dwarfie Hamars, an outcrop of rock on the steep face of the hill behind where it now lies. Inside this block of stone two small cells have been chiselled out, connected by a low narrow passage to an entrance. Alongside lies a large stone that would have originally sealed up the entrance. By tradition, as its name suggests, it was supposed to have been the work of a dwarf, but in 1935 it was established that it is a rock-cut tomb of the late Neolithic period or early Bronze Age, and a similar type of tomb, cut in rock, has been found at Glendalough, Co. Wicklow, in Ireland.

At Skara Brae near the shore of the Bay of Skaill in Sandwick, the walls of some stone houses came to light in the middle of last century, when strong winds accompanied by high tides displaced the sand covering them, and when the site was properly excavated in 1928, seven well-preserved Stone Age houses were discovered. They had been built near or among the sand dune, under which they had eventually been buried, but it is possible that part of this Stone Age village may have been washed away by the Atlantic, which has eaten into the bay. All the houses except one are connected by low and narrow stone-roofed corridors, and although each house is now open to the sky, they would have had some form of roof, maybe made from turf and any branches of trees thrown ashore by waves. In the centre of each main room is a hearth surrounded by a stone kerb, while on either side of the hearth a space for a bed is defined by stone slabs, where heather may have been placed to lie on, and skins used as a bedcover. In the wall above each bed space there is a small recess, probably for the personal possessions of the occupant, and against another wall is a two-storeyed stone structure, probably used to hold household articles. A small stone-lined tank set into the floor may have been used to keep shellfish fresh.

An entrance through the thick walls of each house could be closed by a door, held in place by stone jambs and secured with a bar, and each house was connected to a communal drain. The Skara Brae settlers were evidently of short stature, considering the height of the door frames and also by the size of their beds. A large quantity of sheep and cattle bones, as well as limpet shells, were found among their refuse, indicating that they were herdsmen and shepherds who varied their diet with shellfish. A display of their tools can be viewed on the site.

The Stone Age settlers were followed by an early Bronze Age people who came across the North Sea from Europe and were known as Beaker folk. They were given this name because of the beaker-shaped vessels found in their graves, which may have contained the food and drink thought necessary to sustain the dead on their journey to another world. These early Bronze Age settlers buried their dead individually; their cremated remains contained in a large urn made of clay or steatite, a soft stone found in Shetland but not in Orkney. Sometimes they were buried, also individually, in stone-lined graves which were so small that the body had to be doubled up, their knees drawn up to the chin. As these graves are fairly shallow, they are often found after a plough or some other agricultural implement has disturbed one of the stone slabs covering them. Apart from beakers, stone axe heads and archers' equipment have sometimes been found, buried with the Beaker folk, and it is suggested that they may have been responsible for erecting the standing stone monuments of Brodgar and Stenness, which one would be inclined to associate with the megalithic people.

The standing stone monument at Brodgar is situated on a narrow neck of moorland between Loch Stenness and Loch Harray and takes the form of a wide circle of twenty-seven upright stones of varying heights, the tallest being fifteen feet. Outside this circle, which originally consisted of about sixty stones, is a wide ditch bridged at opposite sides by two crossings. In 1973 archaeological students digging on the south side of the circle to get peat for radio carbon dating, found that the ditch had been cut out of solid rock. This circle of standing stones closely resembles one at Avebury in Wiltshire, which also is surrounded by a ditch.

About a mile down the road, just past the Bridge of Brodgar, are the Stones of Stenness which were known by the local people as the Temple of the Moon. The Stones of Stenness are said to have formed a semicircle of twelve upright stones, perhaps twelve or fifteen feet high. In 1805 there were only five stones standing, and in 1814 some of these were removed by a local farmer for building purposes, which was when the stone of Odin was also removed. This stone, standing a little to the west of the Stones of Stenness, was perforated by a hole through which lovers would join hands to plight their troth. The Stromness pirate, Gow, is said to have become betrothed to a Miss Gordon of Cairston at this stone.

Across the road from the Stones of Stenness is a large monolith known as the Watch Stone, while just beyond the north end of the Bridge of Brodgar, near the road, are two small monoliths. The stone circle of Brodgar is on a promontory which protrudes out into what was once called Loch Stonehouse, probably named after a house called Stonehouse which once stood near the shore of the loch. On a smaller promontory projecting out from the other side of the loch are the few remaining stones of the Stones of Stenness. The Bridge of Brodgar linked the two promontories and this has now been replaced by a causeway which bisects the loch previously known as the Loch of Stonehouse; now the inland part is known as Loch Harray while the other part is Loch Stenness. Stenness derives from the Norse 'Steins-ness', which means the ness of the stones.

The standing stones, erected thousands of years ago, can still create a sensation of awe, and in failing light it wouldn't be difficult to picture a line of white-robed priests or priestesses making their way between the stones on some festive or sacrificial occasion. It has been suggested that stone circles were connected with astronomy. The builders of the Maeshowe tomb had some knowledge of it, for at the winter solstice, and only on this day of the year, the rays of the sun shine along the passage of the tomb. A similar design has been found in a cave temple in Abu Simbel, near Aswan in Upper Egypt, which was built by Ramses II and discovered by the Swiss explorer Jean-Louis Burckhardt at the beginning of the nineteenth century. At the spring and autumn solstices, the rising sun illuminated a statue of the Pharaoh inside the temple, although this may not happen now. The temple was moved to higher ground when the Aswan High Dam was built.

During the Bronze Age climatic conditions began to deteriorate, and in Orkney the inhabitants living on the higher ground abandoned their farmsteads there and moved to more sheltered land near the lochs and the sea. Their deserted farms were eventually covered over with peat. Bronze articles are said to have been scarce in Orkney during the Bronze Age, so the inhabitants must have continued to use bone and stone to make weapons and implements. Towards the end of the Bronze Age, however, a smith settled at Jarlshof in Shetland where he manufactured bronze axes, knives and swords by casting them in clay moulds. Iron is a soft metal compared to bronze, unless it is tempered. When this was discovered, iron, being easy to obtain, soon replaced bronze. The Norse used iron ore which they found in bogs.

Some time during the Iron Age tribes from the continent settled in the east of Scotland, where they built hill forts. Other tribes of a different culture, who may have arrived later, settled in the northern parts of Scotland where they built towers. A broch is the name given by archaeologists to the round, drystone tower built by these settlers. These towers were wide at the base, narrowing towards the top, giving them an appearance resembling present-day cooling towers. The broch at Clickhimin on the southern outskirts of Lerwick in Shetland was built on a small islet in a loch, but can now be reached by a causeway. It is inside a stone wall, built by earlier settlers for defence. A broch was usually situated near fresh water, good farming and pasture land and at a strategic position. The broch builders probably brought the technique of building the towers from their country of origin. There are round towers of some similarity to the broch in the Balearic Islands and Sardinia.

Orkney may have been the centre of a broch kingdom stretching from Caithness to the Shetlands, a kingdom that would have passed to the Picts. Orkney has numerous broch sites, but most as elsewhere are now almost reduced to their foundations. The only complete example in existence is on the isle of Mousa in Shetland, which has probably survived because of its more isolated position. The brochs vary in size, but as their construction is practically consistent, the following description will be typical of most.

A broch is entered by a narrow passageway through a thick base wall. About halfway along this passage, stone jambs are positioned for a stone door, which may have been held in place by a wooden beam, to secure it in the event of an attack. At ground level a number of small cells were positioned in the base wall, while at about eye level two concentric walls rose from it, the inside wall rising vertically, the outer wall curving inwards to make the broch narrower at the top. The outer and inner walls were fixed together by stone slabs at about every five feet of height to form galleries around the broch. These galleries were lit by small openings in the inner wall and were linked by stone steps or stairways leading up to a parapet at about forty feet above ground level, where perhaps a sentry on lookout duty was posted.

The best example of a broch in Orkney is at Midhowe in Rousay, near the Midhowe burial cairn. It stands at a height of fifteen feet, with a diameter at its base of about sixty feet, with a thickness of wall varying from twelve to fifteen feet. It was built on a small promontory between two sea inlets, so it is protected by the sea on three sides, and on the fourth side by two ditches and a massive stone rampart. Along this shore of Rousay are five other broch sites, while on the main island, i.e. the Mainland shore which is on the other side of Eynhallow Sound, there are more, the Gurness broch at Aikerness in Evie being the best example here. This broch rises to the first gallery, and in the circular courtyard is a stone-covered well, while around the broch are the foundations of the type of buildings that archaeologists state were sometimes constructed with stone taken from the towers, indicating that their construction was of a later date. On the landward side, the Gurness broch is protected by two semicircular stone ramparts with ditches. At the entrance to the site there is a small museum.

The Gurness broch is situated in a rather scenic position, for to the west the small isle of Eynhallow rises out of the sea, while across the sound lies Westness, and to the east Trumland House, built by a General Burroughs. When he was a young officer in the Sutherland Highlanders, the general took part in the Crimean War, and a few years later he was present at the siege of Lucknow during the Indian Mutiny. After being wounded at Lucknow, he received further injuries while on the roof of a house which was blown up. While on a visit to Orkney he was made a burgess of Kirkwall, and just before he died in 1905 he was knighted.

The broch men occupied the north of Scotland and the islands, while hill tribes occupied central Scotland, and other tribes would have occupied the eastern coastal region and the Lowlands. The Anglo-Saxon chronicle states that in the year AD 46 Emperor Claudius brought the Orkney Islands under Roman rule. A Jo Ben, writing in 1529 after having visited the islands, stated that the kings of Orkney ruled from Birsay in former days and that Orkney was then subject to Rome as an inscription stone testifies. Birsay in the West Mainland could have been the seat of government at this time, a belief backed up by the large number of broch sites situated around the shores of Eynhallow Sound and in the parish of Harray. The Reverend George Barry mentions a King Gaius who may have ruled at this time. He is said to have been at war with the Romans, but was defeated and taken with his family to Rome as prisoners. In about AD 83, Agricola, the Roman governor of Britain, marched into Scotland and defeated the hill tribes of the central Highlands. According to the Roman writer Tacitus, who recorded the event, the battle took place at Mons Graupius, a location which has never been identified. Agricola then took his fleet to Orkney where he obtained the submission of the people, who, one would think, would have been the broch men. Shortly afterwards Agricola was recalled to Rome, after which the Roman legion in the Highlands was withdrawn to aid troops on the continent. With a shortage of troops it was now difficult to man the northern forts, and these were evacuated accordingly. The Romans slowly retreated south until they eventually reached their Tyne–Solway fortifications where Hadrian's Wall was later built.

After the Roman retreat a number of brochs appeared in the

Lowlands of Scotland. Three of these brochs, north of the Tweed, were built at strategic positions on hilltops to guard the valleys of the Gala and Whiteadder, tributaries of the Tweed. The Tor-woodlee and Bow brochs guarded the valley of the Gala, while the Edin's Hall guarded the valley of the Whiteadder. The Edin's Hall broch was built inside earth-bank and ditch fortifications of a former hilltop fort, and its walls still stand to about five feet high. It is easiest approached from the south-west because the ground falls steeply down to the valley on the east and north sides, where the river curves around the hill. This would give a lookout an unobstructed view over the country which stretches for about seven to eight miles north-east towards the sea.

These brochs north of the Tweed were probably built around AD 100, but there doesn't seem to be sufficient evidence to explain how they appeared so far south. Orkney broch men were then under Roman rule and it is suggested that broch men from the west of Scotland who had an alliance with the hill tribes may have built the Lowland brochs. During the second century the brochs of Scotland were pulled down and huts and houses appeared around the ruins of the broch towers, as at the Gurness site in Orkney.

Some time between when the brochs were dismantled in the second century and when the Norwegians settled in the northern isles in the ninth century, Picts occupied them. There is evidence in a few place names which include the element Petta, which is Norse for Picts. In the north of Shetland there is Pettadale, which means the valley of the Picts, and there is the Pentland Firth between Orkney and Caithness which derives from Pettaland Firth, meaning the Firth of Pictland. During excavations in a graveyard on the Brough of Birsay in 1935, an island on the west coast of Mainland, pieces of a large gravestone were found, which, when pieced together, revealed that carved on it there were what are called Pictish symbols: an eagle, an elephant, a mirror case and a crescent. Below these symbols are what could be three cloaked Pictish warriors, each with a spear and a decorated square shield, and because of the elephant symbol on the stone they could have eastern connections.

In Scotland there was a Pictish province of Fortriu which

consisted of Strathearn and Menteith, while further east Fife might have been another Pictish province, with Abernethy as its capital. By the end of the sixth century after the Romans had left Britain, the Picts had divided themselves into two groups, separated by the Grampian mountains. Brude, king of the northern Picts, had been converted to Christianity by Columba, who made many missionary journeys in the Highlands of Scotland. In about AD 575 Columba was at the court of Brude, thought to have been at Inverness. Brude must have had some authority over Orkney for he gave instructions, which must have been at Columba's request, concerning the safety of Cormac, a missionary who was travelling in northern waters and who was expecting to visit Orkney.

In the year AD 297, a writer describes Picts as attacking the Roman frontier and raiding Roman Britain with the Scots of Dalriada. In AD 367 they raided south again when they swept over Hadrian's Wall. By the end of the seventh century they occupied Scotland from the Firth of Forth to the Shetlands, a region where Pictish symbol stones have been found, but in AD 830, however, they suffered a disastrous defeat at the hands of the Danes, and another when fighting Kenneth MacAlpin, king of the Scots of Dalriada.

It would have been some time after Cormac's visit that the Celtic clergy took up residence, in Orkney, on small isolated islands or at sites difficult to access. Excavations on the Brough of Birsay, an island in the West Mainland, revealed the remains of a Celtic monastery and chapel. Another location where the Celtic clergy chose to reside was the Brough of Deerness, a rocky headland at the eastern tip of Mainland. Here a monastic settlement was established which was reached by a narrow and dangerous path from the shore up the side of a cliff, and in the past pilgrims risked death and injury to visit the ruins of a primitive chapel on the flat top. On Papa Westray and Papa Stronsay in the North Isles, stones with the form of a cross carved on them have been found, which, together with their Norse name-tag Papa, suggests sites of the Celtic clergy. The Norse called the Celtic clergy Papae because of the white robes they wore. Most of the place names in the northern isles today have

Norse origins; the few exceptions, Unst, Yell and Fetlar, the three most northerly isles of Shetland, are said to have pre-Norse names, perhaps Pictish. In some areas of Scotland, so-called inscription stones have been found. These stones sometimes have a Celtic cross and other designs carved on them, and around the edges there are what are called ogam inscriptions. These inscriptions are written in an alphabet which is formed with straight lines, so like the Norse runes they are easy to carve into stone. The ogam alphabet was brought to Scotland by Irish monks.

During the eighth century, Viking sea rovers appeared on the seas of Europe. The outlying islands of Scotland were raided for sheep and cattle and for the gold and silver in the churches. On the islands the sea rovers sometimes took possession of a piece of land that jutted out into the sea and converted it into a pirate stronghold from where they would raid further afield. One of their earliest raids was to Lindisfarne in Northumberland in AD 793, when the church was destroyed and looted and the monks slaughtered. In AD 806 they raided and plundered Iona on the west coast of Scotland, killing sixty-eight members of the community. A hoard of silver articles found under church foundations on St Ninian's Isle in Shetland in 1958 are thought to have been buried there in about AD 800, and were in all probability hidden to keep them safe from marauding Vikings. The Celtic clergy may have fled from the Vikings and many of the Pictish inhabitants of the northern isles may have done the same, leaving behind deserted farms and an almost unpopulated land. The Celts evidently had been sufficiently experienced sailors to have travelled to Iceland, a voyage of four or five days westwards, for when the Norse arrived there during the ninth century, they named a small island off the east coast of that country Papa-ey, i.e. Papae Island, which indicates that the Celtic clergy were or had been living there before the Norse arrived.

When Harald Fairhair of Norway claimed the northern isles, the population is said to have consisted of Norse settlers, most of whom came from south-west Norway, an area which today has friendly links with Orkney.

The Norse Era

Before the time of Harald Fairhair the country we now know as
Norway was composed of small independent states. Those along
the northern coast were linked by a sea route known as the
Norge, i.e. the Northway, and from this sea route Norway got its
name. During the latter half of the ninth century, Harald Fairhair,
ruler of Vestfold, a small state in southern Norway, imposed his
authority on all the other small states. He defeated the last of the
chieftains to oppose him at the sea battle of Hafrsfiord, near
Stavanger, and then united the former independent states he had
conquered into one kingdom. He appointed new chieftains in
place of those he had deposed while the deposed chieftains sailed
with their families and followers to seek new land in the west.
Some settled in Iceland and Ireland, while others took refuge in
the islands and northern Scotland and the Isle of Man, from
where they continued to defy Harald by raiding his dominion.

According to the sagas, one summer Harald Fairhair sailed
west to punish these raiders. He sailed first to Shetland and then
to Orkney, and then on to the Hebrides and the Isle of Man,
annexing much land. In one of the battles, Ivar, one of Jarl
Rognvald of More's sons, was killed, and before returning home
to Norway King Harald gave Orkney and Shetland to Rognvald as
compensation for the loss of his son. Rognvald was the son of
Eystein, jarl of Upplanders in Norway and had been given More
and Romsdale by King Harald as a reward for the help he gave
Harald when fighting the independent chieftains. Rognvald didn't
want the islands so he passed them on to his brother, Sigurd, who
was King Harald's forecastle man, and the king gave Sigurd the
title of jarl, or earl.

Another son of Rognvald of More is claimed to have been the
founder of Normandy, ancestor of the dukes of Normandy and
the Norman kings of England. He was Rolf the Ganger, sometimes known as Rollo, who was so large that no horse could carry

him. After being banished from Norway, Rolf sailed to the Western Isles where there were other refugees from Harald Fairhair, and he led these warriors on Viking raids. Rolf wanted to win land to settle in and, after giving up attempts in England because Alfred the Great was successful in defeating Viking invasions, Rolf tried France. Vikings had been raiding parts of France for almost a hundred years and were sometimes bought off with a Danegeld, a payment of money as a bribe to stop any further plundering. Rolf probably entered northern France by way of the River Seine. In AD 911, outside the walls of the town of Chartres, he came to terms with Charles III, king of France, who gave him a grant of land, and in return Rolf promised the king allegiance. The following year he was baptised. The Reverend George Barry says that King Charles gave him his daughter Gesla in marriage and a province in northern France, to be held by him and his heirs as a feudal duchy. This province or duchy became known as Normandy and its capital Rouen. Rolf had the title of jarl or earl of Rouen, but his descendants became known as the dukes of Normandy. Rolf's tomb is in the cathedral of Rouen which was built later.

When Harald Fairhair became ruler of the small states, he claimed all the odal land for the crown and imposed a land tax (skat) on all cultivated land. The odal land must have been in existence before the time of Harald Fairhair while the laws connected with it are said to resemble those in some eastern countries, which could indicate that the early settlers came from the east. The odal land belonged to the peasants and was inheritable, but could be sold and then redeemed within a certain period of time. The owner of odal land was called an odaller. To calculate the amount of land tax to be paid, a unit called an ounce land or uris land was used. In the land of the Hausa in Nigeria, some time in the past, there was a property tax called zakat, which is somewhat phonetically similar to skat. The zakat was based on the laws of Islam, and as the Norse were in contact with the Arab world around this time, this could have been where the skat originated.

In Norway each chieftain was allowed one-third of the taxes he collected for living and defence purposes, but they had to render military service to Harald, so unlike the previous independent chieftains they were vassals of the king. Harald had claimed all the odal land for the crown, but when his son Hakon became king after deposing his brother, Eric Bloodaxe, he restored the odal land to the peasants for supporting him. This happened in Orkney as well, for the early Norse settlers lived on land that under Norse law would be classed as odal land. When Half Dan, one of King Harald of Norway's sons, was killed in Orkney, King Harald put a fine on the islands which evidently the odallers had to pay. As they were too poor to pay it, the earl paid the fine on the condition that the landowners gave their land to him. In about AD 991, Sigurd, an earl of Orkney, gave this land back to the heirs in return for their help when a Scottish earl who had challenged him in Caithness was defeated. From the time of Turf Einar the Orkney earls were permitted to keep the whole of the skat for administrative and defence purposes, and the Orkney earls were more independent and responsible only to a distant sovereign.

In Norway, at the beginning of the Viking period, pagan feasts were held on fixed dates, sometimes accompanied by sacrifices to appease the gods. These pagan customs came to an end in about AD 1000 when Olaf Tryggvason, a descendant of Harald Fairhair, returned to Norway. He claimed the throne of Norway and as he had been baptised abroad he converted the country to Christianity. His successor, Olaf II, is said to have been baptised in Rouen while serving with the duke of Normandy. Normandy had been Christianised after Rolf the Ganger was baptised there in AD 912. Sigurd the Crusader, a king in south Norway at the beginning of the twelfth century, took sixty ships to Constantinople, once called Byzantium, and fought Moors on the way. In the middle of the twelfth century Earl Rognvald of Orkney went on a crusade, fought Moors, and also visited Constantinople.

Constantinople was named after the Roman Emperor Constantine the Great and was a centre of Christianity for over a thousand years until it was captured by the Turks in AD 1453. Norsemen served as mercenaries in the Varangians, the emperor's special troops. Harald Hardrada served with them and amassed a fortune before returning to Norway to claim the throne. At this time Constantinople was a city of some splendour and importance, as it was the capital of the rich Byzantine emperors. It had magnificent churches and palaces, statues, columns and obelisks, gilded roofs and long streets which were lit at night, all of which impressed everyone who visited it. Chariot-racing and games took place at a hippodrome which was adorned by the replica of a chariot and four horses abreast made from an alloy of copper, gold and silver. These horses can now be seen in St Mark's Square, Venice, where they were taken when Constantinople was sacked and captured by crusaders in AD 1204. When the Emperor Michael Palaeologus of Byzantium recovered the city in AD 1262 most of the valuable treasures had either been carried away or destroyed and chariot-racing had ceased. The Norse Vikings roamed the seas as far away as Spain and the western Mediterranean, so the sea route used by the Norsemen to reach Byzantium would have been an extension of a familiar route. The impression one gets when reading of it is that it wasn't anything unusual. By the date of Earl Rognvald's crusade the Norse had colonised Iceland and Greenland and had presumably reached America.

When the Vikings arrived in the northern isles, the Celtic clergy who were established there fled, and it wasn't until Earl Thorfinn Sigurdson founded his church at Birsay in the middle of the eleventh century that Christianity was introduced again. Thorfinn's father, Sigurd II, had been forcibly converted by Olaf Tryggvason, but he returned to his pagan beliefs when his son died in Norway where he had been taken by Olaf. There in a church on the island of Egilsay with an unusual round tower which could have been built by the Celtic clergy before the Norse arrived – it resembles similar structures built in Ireland at this time. It is known as the church of St Magnus, and Earl Magnus may have prayed here on the day before he met his death on the island. In the nineteenth century when families were evacuated from the island of Eynhallow, which lies midway between Rousay and Mainland, it was discovered that the building they had occupied was actually a church dating from the twelfth century, and as the Norse named the island *Eyin helga*, meaning 'holy island', which is the same name they gave to the island of Iona, it could have been the site of a Celtic church. An early church at Kirkwall which was dedicated to King Olaf II of Norway, who after his death was declared a saint, was probably built by Earl Rognvald Brusison.

Just inside the gateway of the Orphir churchyard is a renovated fragment of a round church which was probably built by Earl Haken Paulson on his return from a pilgrimage to Jerusalem early in the twelfth century. All that remains of it today is an apse, the remainder having been demolished in the eighteenth century to make room for a parish church, now also demolished. On the islands of Westray and Wyre there are also ruins of twelfth-century churches.

Kali Kolson, who changed his name to Rognvald, vowed to build a stone minster in Kirkwall in memory of his uncle Earl Magnus if he succeeded in a claim for a share of the earldom, which he accomplished in AD 1136. One year later the foundations were laid and the building was started in a style of architecture known as Norman. Norman architecture is distinguished by thick walls, small windows, rounded arches and massive round pillars which all help to give the interior an impression of great strength and age, By the early thirteenth century, however, Gothic architecture was taking the place of Norman, and the building of the minster was continued in this style. A semicircular Norman apse at the east end was pulled down so that the choir could be enlarged and a large Gothic window was built in the east gable. The foundations of the Norman apse were discovered under the floor of the choir during restoration work. In the eighteenth century bone remains found nine feet up in one of the pillars of the choir were thought to be those of St Magnus, but in 1919 some other bones were found in an opposite pillar.[1] These showed that the skull had been split by a blow from a sharp instrument so they are almost certain to be those of St Magnus, while these found earlier in the eighteenth century are probably those of St Rognvald, the founder of the cathedral. The top of the bell tower, built in the fourteenth century, can be reached by a spiral stairway from the transepts, as can the triforium of the nave, where there are various antique objects of interest. At the west end, three pointed arched door-

---

[1] The oak box which had contained the relics of St Magnus can be seen in the Tankerness House Museum, Kirkwall.

ways which form the main entrance are early Gothic, and also at this end of the cathedral, the foundations of two towers were discovered in the twentieth century.

Stavanger Cathedral in Norway is thought to have been built just after St Magnus Cathedral in Kirkwall, in the same style and by the same builders. It is smaller but has, at the front, the two towers which were abandoned during the building of St Magnus Cathedral. St Magnus Cathedral is built mainly of local red sandstone.

Earl Thorfinn visited Rome in about AD 1050, and on his return built Christ Church at Birsay and established there the first bishop's see in the Orkneys. Joseph Anderson, writing in the introduction of the *Orkneyinga Saga*, which he edited, says that in the past foundations of a church known as Christ Kirk lay beside the parish church of Birsay, but modern opinion favours church foundations on the Brough of Birsay as being those of Thorfinn's Christ Church. In the twelfth century a cathedral was built at Trondheim in Norway to contain the tomb of Olaf II after he had been declared a saint, and a cardinal from Rome ordained an archbishop at the new Trondheim Cathedral and the Orkney see was placed under his charge. At the beginning of the twelfth century it is stated that the archbishop of York had jurisdiction over the Orkney bishops. William the Old, who is recorded as being the first bishop of Orkney, may have been appointed by the archbishop of York and then allowed to stay in office under the new arrangement. William the Old died in AD 1168 and was succeeded by another William who died in AD 1188. The next bishop was Bjarni, son of chieftain Kolbein Hruga, a Norwegian who resided on the island of Wyre in about AD 1150. It was during his time that the remains of Earl Rognvald found a resting place in the cathedral that he had founded. Bjarni was descended through his mother from Paul I, and is described as a poet and diplomat. He died in AD 1223. Then there was a Bishop Jofreyr, who would have been in office when Earl John, who is called the last of the Norse earls, was murdered in Thurso.

In Norse times the main farm of a district was called a *bu*, and was the residence of a chieftain or goding as he was known after the eleventh century. The bu of Orphir was one of the residences used by the Norse earls, and the foundations of the earl's drinking hall, which was the stage for some dramatic events as recorded in the sagas, can be seen just outside the gate of the Orphir churchyard. It was near here, in the Midland haven or harbour, that King Hakon of Norway laid up his warship and part of his fleet on returning from the Battle of Largs. The chieftains owed the earl allegiance and, in an emergency, when warning beacons were lit on the hills, smoke by day and fire at night, a chieftain would bring his longship to a rendezvous, crewed with the armed warriors from the district he administered. The beacons were situated on the highest hills, now called Ward Hills, a corruption of the Old Norse *warth*, meaning beacon. A beacon at Fair Isle could be seen from North Ronaldsay in Orkney, and when Rognvald Kolson was waiting in Shetland while on his way to claim his share of the earldom, his father Kol deceived the lookout on Fair Isle into believing that Rognvald was sailing for Orkney, and the lookout lit his beacon. This alerted the chieftains in Orkney who would have manned their longships on a false alarm, but when Rognvald sailed later, Kol put a man on Fair Isle to soak the beacon so that no warning could be given, allowing Rognvald to reach Orkney without any opposition.

It is estimated that Orkney had about sixteen longships, probably with twenty or twenty-five oars each side, and the earl possibly had one with thirty oars each side. The longship is considered to have been very unseaworthy, although long journeys were undertaken in them. Voyages to Iceland, Greenland and the North American coast weren't made in longships but in the knorr, a trading vessel which was more suitable for sailing in open water. The knorr, like the longship, was clinker-built,[2] double-ended, with one square sail and like the longship used oars as an auxiliary power, and had a side rudder called a steer board, which gave its name to the starboard side of a vessel. She had broad beams, a shallow draught and a larger displacement than the longship, which must have made her more seaworthy. When a storm blew up at Largs, King Hakon of Norway suffered severe losses to his fleet of longships.

---

[2] The planking on the sides of the boat overlaps downwards on the outside.

Before the Norsemen took to deep-sea voyaging they used boats for fishing in home waters and for coastal trips along the Norge (or Northway) which was sheltered by many offshore islands. The Picts were seafaring people and they traded regularly with Norway until the end of the eighth century. The Norse could have gleaned information from them about how to build seagoing ships and the places they sailed to, because when the Norse took to voyaging overseas they followed routes used by the Picts. Navigation was then primitive, the North Star and the sun being used to plot a position.

During the ninth century, Floki Vilgerdarson, a Viking, sailed from Shetland to Iceland. As he had no sailing directions, it is claimed that he took some ravens with him to help in the navigation. After he had left the Faeroe islands well behind, Floki freed one of the ravens and it flew off in the direction of the Faeroes. A day later he released another and it flew high in the sky, then returned and perched on the mast, evidently having seen no land. The following day it rose to a great height and flew off in a westerly direction and Floki set his course in the direction the bird had taken and came to the coast of Iceland.

The Norse dialect known as Norn, which was spoken in Orkney, could have had its roots in south-west Norway where the Norse settlers who came to Orkney probably belonged, which explains why Orkney has developed a friendship with Hordaland in that part of Norway. Some of the speakers on Radio Norway have a manner of speaking which resembles Orcadian. Danska, a dialect sometimes referred to, seems likely to have developed when Denmark had the sovereignty of the islands before they were transferred to Scotland. By then Lowland Scottish had been introduced by Scottish bishops and later by Scottish earls who had been appointed by Denmark and their Scottish servants. By the seventeenth century most of the inhabitants were bilingual and although in about 1700 Norn (and possibly Danska also) was still being spoken in some parishes, by 1750 any Scandinavian dialect had virtually died out.

Words of Norse origin, however, continued to be used and the following are a few: flit, which derives from Old Norse *flytja*. In Shetland a flit-boat was used to ferry animals from the shore to a ship anchored offshore; in Orkney it was used in connection with moving cows to a fresh piece of grazing; it was also used, probably further south, in connection with moving from one house to another. Kirn, from Old Norse *kirna*, is a churn for making butter. Kist or kyst from Old Norse *kista* is a chest, a strong wooden box. Kye from Old Norse *kyr* seems to have been used for more than one cow, while a single cow appears to have been called a coo. Kirk from Old Norse *kirkja* is a church. Peedie, meaning small, is probably a variant of *peerie*, e.g. the Peerie Sea, Kirkwall.

The surname Flett originated in the Norse period. A Thorkel Flettir of Westray is mentioned in the *Orkneyinga Saga*. In the Norse period a person was sometimes spoken of as Harald, son of Magnus, and sometimes as Harald Magnus's son. If Harald Magnus's son had a son called Eric he would have been known as Eric, son of Harald, or Eric Harald's son. Sweyn Asliefsson, the great Viking chief of Gairsay, was evidently known as the son of his mother, Aslief, instead of his father, Olaf. At some stage the second name must have stuck as Magnusson became a surname in Iceland. In Orkney it became Manson while the Christian name Magnus sometimes became Mansie. One of the meanings of son is a descendant, which will be what surnames like Magnusson mean and will be similar to the meaning of Mac in Scottish surnames. Some Orkney families took a farm or place name as a surname, which was a custom common in Scotland. A William of Abernethy and a John of Menteith signed the Declaration of Arbroath in 1320. Later the preposition 'of' was dropped, and these persons would then have been known as William Abernethy and John Menteith. This type of surname is territorial and is said to have come to Orkney with the Scottish settlers, and the following are some of those that have evolved there: Brough, Corrigal, Garson, Hourston, Kirkness, Linklater, Marwick, Norquoy, Scarth, Twatt and Windwick.

Most place names in the northern isles have Scandinavian origins, but their spellings have become altered over the years, sometimes through a mistake in the interpretation of the meaning. One example of this is Kirkwall, which was originally Kirkjavagr, Old Norse for 'bay of the kirk' and the kirk referred to is most likely to be the church built by Earl Rognvald Brusison in memory of King Olaf of Norway. This church, probably made of wood, was known as St Olaf's Kirk. Today an ornamented stone doorway can be seen built into St Olaf's Wynd off Bridge Street, Kirkwall, probably taken from the last St Olaf's Church on or near the site of the early one which was thereabouts. *Vagr*, the ending of Kirkjavagr, became distorted into *waa* as the years passed and as this resembled the Scottish *wa* for wall, it became Kirkwall. The same thing happened to Walls in Hoy, which was previously spelt Waas or Waiss, both meaning a number of bays.

A -by ending is considered to be evidence of very early settlement and for an example of this in Orkney, I suggest Yesnaby. In some parts of England where the Danes settled this ending can also be found. On the east coast there is Whitby and at the mouth of the Humber Grimsby, while further inland there is Selby. Grimsby must have been settled by a settler called Grim, as Graemsay in Orkney was, for in Old Norse this island was Grimsay, i.e. Grim's Island. In the northern isles there are also farms of very early origin said to have had the -by ending, so in some cases a district may have been given the same name as an early farm settlement.

Early farms can also be identified by the endings of their names, and the following are some considered to be of early origin. The most common of this group is -bister, which comes from the old Norse *bolstathr*, meaning farmstead, and for an example from the many farm names with this ending I chose Swanbister in the parish of Orphir. Situated in a fertile area, near the site of a broch and a sheltered bay on the edge of Scapa Flow, it could well be of early origin. Another farm name ending which could indicate an early farm is -setter, which could derive from either of two Old Norse elements, i.e. *setr*, meaning a homestead, or *saetr*, mountain pasture. In Norway the cattle is taken to a *seter* in the hills for summer grazing. Grimsetter in St Ola parish, which will be named after another Grim, is where Kirkwall airport is sited and is low ground so is likely to have been a homestead. Winksetter situated on the slopes of the Harray hills could have got its name ending through originally being summer grazing land.

The house of Winksetter is still standing and dates from the fourteenth century or earlier. It is built with all the features of a Norse farm dwelling and has the usual free-standing fire back in the living room, on one side of which the peat fire was built. In a wall there is a place for a quern hand mill which was used for grinding grain, and at floor level a goose nest. A sae-bink, a projecting stone forming a shelf, was for the sae, which was a water tub, so the bink would be the projecting stone. The water tub had two lugs with holes through which a stick called a sae-tree was passed, so that two people could carry it between them. Cogs in which ale is passed around at weddings appear to be miniature versions of the sae.

Old Norse *garthr* means an enclosure and when this is used as a farm name ending it becomes -gar and -garth; but besides meaning that the farm was enclosed with a dyke, it may have sometimes meant that it was near a township dyke. Brodgar in Stenness is probably an example of the -gar ending, meaning that the farm was enclosed with a dyke for it is surrounded by moorland and standing stones. Old Norse *bru* means a bridge and this forms the first part of Brodgar, so in Norse times there must have been some form of bridge there, probably linking Brodgar and the standing stones with the road to Kirkwall and Stromness, as a causeway does today. Garth, a remote farm just north of the old township dyke of Outertown, Stromness, could have got its name because of it being near the old dyke or garth of Outertown.

Skaill is another common farm name in Orkney, but it doesn't appear to be so in Shetland. Skaill is said to derive from the Old Norse *skali*, meaning a hut or shed, but in Orkney it is thought to have meant a hall. In Norway where wood is plentiful, the meaning, a shed, would have been appropriate, but in Orkney where wood was scarce it may have taken on a different meaning, such as a simple stone building. On the map of Orkney all the Skaill farm or place names are near the shore, which must have some significance. Some farms had something on their land or nearby that neighbouring farms didn't, such as a burial mound, a broch or, as in Brodgar, a bridge, and this was used in their farm names. Skaill farms evidently had a skali nearby and took this for a name. By using a little imagination one could suppose that the skali was used to house the sails and oars of a longship and maybe as a drinking place for the crew. This would account for a skali meaning a hall in Orkney, for some chieftains had drinking halls for their men, and this would also account for the Skaill farms being near the shore. There is a farm called Skaill in the island of Egilsay, and a short distance from it there is a Skaill Taing, a tongue of land or rock which juts out into the sea. A pier is built on to this now, so it must be a suitable landing place for boats. There is a Bay of Skaill and a farm called Skaill on the northern tip of Westray, and in Rousay a Geo of Skaill, a narrow opening in the cliffs. In Sandwick, on the west coast of Mainland, there is another farm called Skaill which is also near a Bay of Skaill, but these rather contradict the idea that Skaill names are connected with a harbour for boats, for the Bay of Skaill has no protection from the westerly gales which frequently sweep in from the Atlantic. This Skaill would fit in better with the Reverend George Barry's version of its meanings which is that it implies a situation at the seaside exposed to the noise of the billows. On the island of Gairsay there is a farm called Langskaill which was the home of the chieftain Sweyn Asliefsson. Near the shore there is a low house sixty feet long which is considered to have originally been Sweyn's drinking hall, which the saga says was the largest in Orkney. The farm of Langskaill (Long skali) could have taken its name from the long drinking hall.

Old Norse *kvi* means an enclosure for cattle, and it becomes -quoy when used as a farm name ending. Most farms with a -quoy ending were untaxed, which maybe was because they were of late origin and only came into existence after the period when skat was being imposed, or maybe because they were only used for cattle which may not have justified a land tax being imposed on them.

The original farm of a settlement would have been situated in a fertile area, and as the years passed it would have been divided up among the family according to the odal law of Norway, so a town or tunship would have been formed about it. Sometimes a portion of a farm was given the name of the original farm with a prefix added to it to indicate its position relative to the original farm dwelling. For example, if the original farm was called Biggin, and a son had inherited part of it, he would build a house there, and could have called it Upper, Mid or Lower Biggin. Around a tunship was a dyke built of stones, sods of earth and grass roots, to separate the cultivated land from the moorland, and the animals were kept inside this dyke during the winter, but were allowed outside to graze during the summer. In some parts of Scotland, possibly in places where stone was scarce, there were dykes made of sods alone, and these were known as fail dykes. A fail is most likely a thin sod, while a thick sod is called a divot. Divots were probably more suitable for building a dyke of stones and sods, as they would fit in better with the size of the stones, while a dyke built entirely of sods would possibly stand up better if made of thin sods, i.e. fails or feals. In Scotland a tunship was called a clachan, and the animals were taken for the summer to a nearby hill to graze. These hill grazings were known as shielings, the equivalent of the Norwegian seter, and here the womenfolk lived during the summer months, passing the time spinning and making butter and cheese. Every owner of land in a tunship evidently had a piece of land near his house which was his own possession and was called his toomal. There was also communal land, and some of this was divided up into strips for growing corn. These strips of arable land were separated by strips of grassland called merkesters, a word that lives on as the name of a hotel near Dounby in the parish of Harray, which was once the home of Eric Linklater, the writer. This method of dividing the land was known as runrig, but as each owner had got pieces of land which were scattered throughout the tunship it was a very inefficient way of farming. Pieces of tunship dykes are still standing today and one piece can be seen in the parish of Firth, near the old tunship of Redland.

Most Orkney place and farm names contain elements of Scandinavian origin and the following are a selection: *brekka*, a slope, is the origin of the farm names Breck, Brecks, Breckness, Breckan and Brockan, and also the place name Breck Ness; *borg* is a place of defence such as a broch, and is found in Brough, Burrian and, if an island, Burray. *Dalr*, a valley, becomes dale, which will be found in Scorradale. An *eyrr* is a sand or gravel bank and becomes ayre. At Kirkwall an ayre was formed, almost cutting off a piece of the harbour. The gap would have been bridged for the Ayre Road was built over it. There is now an Ayre Hotel there. *Fiall*, a hill, becomes fea as in Leafea, in Stromness parish; *gata*, a road, and *gnipa*, a steep rock or headland are both found in Gaitnip in St Ola; *grind*, a gate, forms the first part of Grindally in Orphir, while *haugr*, a hill or mound, becomes howe, as in Maeshowe. When a farm is in the proximity of a mound it sometimes has this element in its name. *Holmr* is a small island, e.g. Lamb Holm; it can also mean low-lying ground, so maybe the parish of Holm got its name because it is low lying. *Hopr* becomes hope, a sea inlet, e.g. St Margaret's Hope. These seem to be confined to the south isles. *Klettr* means a rock, a rock at the shore, a rocky bank or a cliff. The last part of the name Linkletter, now Linklater, could be this element, and if the first part was from *lyng*, which is heather, the whole could mean a rocky heather bank. *Kuml* means something of antiquity, such as a burial mound, and it becomes cummi as in Cumminess in Stenness. *Myr*, marshy ground, becomes mire, which could be the origin of the farm name Myre. *Oss*, the estuary of a stream, becomes oyce. Oyce is also used where a stretch of water has a narrow entrance to the sea, such as that caused by the build-up of a sand bank. This happened at Kirkwall and the oyce was later cut off from the sea when the Ayre Road was built, and it became the Peerie Sea, meaning small sea. *Sker* is a skerry or a rock in the sea, e.g. Auskerry; *stakkr* a high rock in the sea. Such a rock is known as a stack, e.g. the Stacks of Duncansby, but in Orkney they seem to be called castles, e.g. the Castle of Yesnaby. *Sund*, a narrow passage of water, becomes sound, e.g. Hoy Sound; *tangi*, a tongue of land, becomes taing, which is a name usually given to pieces of the shore, e.g. Scara Taing. A scara is a young gull, so maybe pieces of the shore bearing this name are breeding places for gulls. *Tjorn*, a small loch, becomes chun as in the Loch of Loomachun in Rousay; *vagr* is a sea inlet or bay. *Vik* is also a bay and this becomes wick, e.g. Rackwick in Hoy. In Shetland many of the sea inlets are called voes. *Voe* is stated as being Gaelic so it could be pre-Norse like the island names of Yell, Fetlar and Unst in northern Shetland. An -a and an -ay ending signifies an island. Flotta, which derives from the Old Norse name Flatey, i.e. Flat Island, is an example of an -a ending, while Westray from Old Norse *vestrey*, i.e. 'west island', is an example of an -ay ending. Exceptions are Eynhallow from Old Norse *Eyin helga*, i.e. 'holy island', and Hoy from the Old Norse name *Ha-ey*, which means 'high island'. Eynhallow has the part of its name that means island at the beginning while Hoy has it at the end in the usual way. All of these syllables which mean island will derive from Old Norse *ey*.

There doesn't seem to be much archaeological evidence of the early Scandinavian settlement in Orkney. Viking period houses have been found on the Brough of Birsay, at the broch site at Gurness in Evie and more recently at Buckquoy in Birsay. At Jarlshof in Shetland, however, excavations have revealed a farming settlement with longhouse and outbuildings dated at from AD 800 to 850. Like many excavated in Scandinavia the long walls of the longhouse curve in slightly at their ends, a shape that is said to have derived from the practice of using an upturned boat as a shelter, after having hollowed out the ground underneath to give extra height. This farm settlement used one of its outbuildings as a byre, but other settlements, probably those of the chief's followers, have a portion of the long single room of the longhouse partitioned off to accommodate the cattle. This was a forerunner of later farmhouses. The longhouse excavated at Jarlshof was seventy feet long by twenty feet wide and had walls about five feet thick, and would have been slightly larger than Sweyn's drinking hall on Gairsay. The walls would be built of drystone as wood, the material commonly used in the longhouses in Scandinavia, was a scarce commodity in the northern isles. The roof had been supported on posts and rafters made probably of driftwood from the shore or any timber that was available. The one-room interior where the owner could feast and entertain his friends would have a stone fireplace in the centre and part of the floor raised for sleeping accommodation. This is the typical style of a longhouse which had belonged to a Norse chieftain.

In the valley of the Thjorsa in South Iceland, the great hall of a saga-age farm was excavated in 1939. During the twelfth century it had been buried under ash when Mount Hekla, a nearby volcano, erupted. This farm had belonged to a Gauk Trandilson, who is mentioned in one of the Maeshowe runic inscriptions, which, when deciphered, read: 'These runes were carved by the man best skilled in runes west of the ocean, with the axe which belonged to Gauk Trandilson in South Iceland.'

The Norse Earls

Rognvald, son of Eystein, the jarl of Upplanders in Norway, was descended through Halfdan[1] the Stingy, from the Yngling dynasty of kings from which Harald Fairhair himself was descended. He helped Harald conquer Norway and as a reward got the revenues of More and Romsdale. When Harald sailed west to punish raiders who were plundering his kingdom, Ivar, a son of Rognvald, was killed as stated in the previous chapter, and Harald gave Rognvald the Orkney and Shetland Islands as compensation, and Rognvald gave these to his brother Sigurd.

Sigurd was a great warrior who went campaigning with Thorstein the Red, son of Olaf the White, a Norse ruler of Dublin, and together they subjugated more than half of Scotland. In this campaign Sigurd killed Maelbrigd, a Scottish mormaer,[2] and in bravado tied his victim's head to his saddle bow. While urging his horse forward he scratched his leg on a tooth projecting from the head, which caused Sigurd's death by blood poisoning. He is said to be buried in a mound or cairn on the north bank of the Dornoch Firth and his son Guttorm succeeded him.

After Sigurd's death, Thorstein the Red ruled as king over their conquered lands until AD 875 when he was slain in Caithness by the Scots. Thorstein's mother, Aud the Deep-Minded, gave his daughter Groa in marriage to Duncan, a mormaer in Caithness, then she sailed to Iceland where she spent the rest of her life spreading the gospel among the Norse settlers there.

Sigurd's son Guttorm was earl for only one winter and died childless. The next earl appointed by Harald of Norway was Hallad, another son of Rognvald of More, but he soon relinquished the task and returned home to a more peaceful life on the

---

[1] Halfdan could mean 'half-Danish'.

[2] A mormaer could have been a chieftain appointed by the king to defend his area against invasion.

land, because the islands were a refuge for Vikings.

Einar, a younger brother of Hallad, was then chosen as the next earl. He is said to have been ugly, one-eyed and unloved at home. His father gave him a longboat, and Einar sailed for Shetland. Danish Vikings had taken up residence on the islands and these he killed before taking possession of the earldom. Back in Norway two of Harald's many sons burnt alive the ageing Rognvald of More in his homestead in Norway and one Halfdan came to Orkney and drove Einar from the islands. Earl Einar collected some ships in Scotland and returned to engage Halfdan in a fierce sea battle in the North Ronaldsay Firth. When all was lost Halfdan leapt overboard and the next morning he was seen on North Ronaldsay, the most northern of the Orkney Islands, where he was captured and slain. The earl had Halfdan buried under a cairn of stones and he sang a verse in celebration of having avenged the death of his father, Rognvald of More, at the hands of Halfdan and his brother Gudrod.

In those days it was the custom for the king to demand the death penalty or compensation for a killing, so King Harald sailed to Orkney with his fleet and Einar fled to Scotland again. Harald made the islanders swear fealty to him and he later became reconciled with Einar who got his lands returned to him on payment to Harald of sixty gold marks[3] in compensation for the killing of Halfdan.

Earl Einar was known as Turf Einar for the reason that he cut peat in Scotland because fuel was scarce in the islands. He lived for a long time and died in his bed, and his three sons, Arnkell, Erlend and Thorfinn succeeded him and shared the earldom between them.

Harald Fairhair, king of Norway, was succeeded by one of his sons, Eric Bloodaxe, who was forced into exile a few years later by a younger brother. Eric fled to Orkney where he got men for war expeditions and by AD 948 he was king of the partly Christianised kingdom of York. Within a few years he was driven out of York and then probably returned to Orkney, for in about the year AD 954 the Orkney earls, Arnkell and Erlend, accompanied him

---

[3] A mark was a unit of weight used for gold and silver.

south, leaving their brother Thorfinn to rule the islands, and the two earls and Eric were killed in Northumbria. Eric's queen Gunnhild and her family had gone with him to Orkney, and before they left Ragnhild, Gunnhild's daughter, married Thorfinn's son Arnfinn.

Thorfinn was married to Grelod, daughter of Duncan, mormaer of Duncansby in Caithness, and when he died Thorfinn was buried in South Ronaldsay; he left five sons: Arnfinn, Havard, Hlodver, Liot and Skuli. Ragnhild, who married Arnfinn, the eldest son, now steps into the limelight. After killing her husband at Murkle in Caithness she married his brother, Havard, who then became earl. When she tired of Havard she persuaded his nephew, Einar Klining, to slay him on the promise of marriage and, after the deed was done in Stenness, Ragnhild denied giving Einar any promise and urged another nephew, Einar Hardchaft, to avenge the earl's murder. When this was done, Ragnhild married the third brother, Liot, who removed Einar Hardchaft from the scene. Liot became earl, while another brother, Skuli, was given the earldom of Caithness by the king of Scots, and he also claimed the islands. Skuli was defeated and slain by Liot in Caithness, and Liot then took possession of Caithness; while defending it against the Scots he was wounded and died soon after. The last brother, Hlodver, then became earl and he married a princess of Ireland, the country where their son Sigurd was to meet his death. Hlodver died in Caithness and was buried there in the present-day parish of Watten.

Sigurd, known as 'The Stout', became earl in about AD 980 and was also a great warrior. He held Caithness against the Scots, and harried further south and in the Hebrides and Ireland besides. When a Scottish earl invaded Caithness with a large force, Earl Sigurd asked the Orkneymen for their help. They agreed and Sigurd consulted his Irish mother who made him a banner which when held in the wind resembled a raven in flight. This she said would bring him victory, so with the charmed banner held aloft they went to meet the Scottish earl and, after three standard-bearers fell, Sigurd's mother's prophecy was fulfilled.

In AD 995 Olaf Tryggvason, a descendant of Harald Fairhair, was returning from a Viking cruise during which he had received a rich Danegeld or peace pledge from the English king. During this cruise he had been converted to Christianity and now he intended to convert Norway where they still worshipped heathen gods such as Thor and Odin. In the Orkneys Olaf found Earl Sigurd aboard his ship at Osmondwall in the south of Hoy and threatened him with death and destruction for his earldom if he and the Orkneymen didn't accept the Christian faith. When Sigurd hesitated, Olaf seized the earl's young son, Hundi, and threatened to decapitate him with his sword if Sigurd refused, and under these threats Sigurd submitted. Olaf took Hundi to Norway as a hostage but after a few years Hundi died so Sigurd paid no further allegiance to Olaf.

At Yuletide AD 1013 Earl Sigurd was at his hall in Orphir, feasting and entertaining. His guests included his brother-in-law, Earl Gilli of the Hebrides, King Sigtrygg of Dublin and a party of Icelanders who had been exiled for the crime of burning Njal Thorgeirsson and his family in their homestead in Iceland. Gunnar Lambason, of the Icelanders, was relating to the company his version of the burning, when Kari Solmundarson, a son-in-law of Njal, burst into the hall. Kari had learnt of the whereabouts of the exiles whom he was seeking for revenge and had sailed to Orkney. He arrived at the door of the earl's hall just as Gunnar was telling his story and, when he heard the lies that Gunnar was telling, Kari drew his sword, ran up to the storyteller and struck off his head. Gunnar's head fell on the table at which the earl and his guests were seated and Sigurd ordered Kari to be seized and put to death, but no one moved to carry out the order for they all thought he had done what he had a right to do. Kari and his men left the hall unhindered, boarded their ship and sailed for Caithness where they stayed for a long time with a man called Skeggi of Freswick.

Back at the earl's hall the table was scrubbed, then King Sigtrygg stated the reason for his visit. He had come to ask for Earl Sigurd's help to fight the Christian King Brian Boru, who had defeated most of the Irish chieftains and was now recognised as king of Ireland. King Sigtrygg's mother had been married to King Brian Boru, but they had now separated and she had urged her son Sigtrygg to ask for Sigurd's help to overthrow her former husband. Although reluctant at first, Sigurd finally agreed on the promise of a handsome reward which unfortunately he was not to receive. Earl Sigurd arrived in Dublin on Palm Sunday AD 1014, leaving the three sons by his first marriage in charge of Orkney and sending a younger son, Thorfinn, to the court of the Scottish king, who was Thorfinn's grandfather. The battle took place at Clontarf near Dublin and the Norsemen followed the same raven banner which had brought them victory in Caithness, but fate had decreed otherwise this time, for after a long and bloody struggle Earl Sigurd was slain and the Norse fled. King Brian was slain by a Viking chief called Brodir as he prayed in a wood after his victory, but Brodir foolhardily spread the news that he had killed the king and he was pursued and captured, then suffered an agonising death by having his belly slit and his intestines wound round an oak tree. Any hope of a Scandinavian-dominated Ireland was now ended and King Sigtrygg died a monk in the monastery on Iona.

It is related that on the day of the battle a man in Caithness saw a number of riders approach a small hill near his home and disappear inside it. Out of curiosity he went near the spot and through an opening in the side of the hill he saw twelve women busy weaving. As they weaved they sang a mournful ode describing the battle and foretelling the deaths of King Brian and the earl of Orkney. This traditional ode was translated from the Danish language into Latin and from this Thomas Gray wrote his famous 'Ode of the Fatal Sisters', the sisters being Valkyries who, according to Scandinavian mythology, select those destined for slaughter and conduct them to Valhalla, the hall of Odin.

After Sigurd's death, his three sons, Sumarlidi, Brusi and Einar divided the earldom between themselves, while Thorfinn, who had been left under the care of his grandfather, Malcolm of Scotland, got Caithness and Sutherland from the Scottish king, with the title of earl. Thorfinn grew up to be tall and strong and is also said to have been ugly and greedy, but he was skilful in battle. Sumarlidi soon died and Einar took his share of the isles. Einar was constantly going on Viking expeditions for which he levied men from the landowners who resented this because their farms suffered. At the next assembly or *thing*, where disputes were settled, Thorkel, son of Amandi of Sandwick in Deerness, complained on behalf of the landowners and the earl promised to cut his expeditions by half. The earl was angry at having his activities criticised, so Thorkel left the islands on the advice of his father and went to Caithness where he became foster father to the young Thorfinn, and because of this became known as Thorkel Fostri.

Although he was earl of Caithness and Sutherland, when he came of age Thorfinn demanded a share of Orkney, but a peace was arranged and Thorfinn got a third of the Orkneys. He appointed his own deputies there and lived in Caithness while Brusi and Einar joined their portions together. Earl Thorfinn sent Thorkel Fostri to the isles to collect revenues; he returned in a hurry when he heard that Earl Einar intended killing him, so he went to Norway for safety and spent the winter there.

During the summers Earl Einar ravaged Scotland and Ireland and one summer he was heavily defeated because Eyvind, a Norwegian baron, and his men had assisted the Irish. On his way back to Norway bad weather forced Eyvind to seek shelter in the islands, and on learning this Earl Einar got his revenge by killing him, a deed that greatly displeased King Olaf Haraldsson of Norway. The Norwegian king sent for Thorfinn, who returned to the islands from Norway in a large, fully equipped warship given to him by the Norwegian king. Thorfinn and Thorkel prepared to do battle with Einar, but Brusi intervened and acted as peace-maker. Einar also became reconciled with Thorkel Fostri and two feasts were arranged. The first was at Thorkel's house in Sand-wick, Deerness, and when it was time to ride to the earl's hall for the second feast, Thorkel became suspicious and sent out scouts along the road where they found three parties of armed men waiting to ambush them. On hearing this Thorkel delayed his departure and when he got the opportunity Thorkel killed Earl Einar with a blow on the head with his axe as the earl sat near the fire. Thorkel and his men rode off and then sailed to Norway where King Olaf, when he heard of the deed, was well pleased and they spent the winter there. The year that Einar died was AD 1020 and Brusi took possession of Einar's portion of the islands, for they had made a pact that when one died the survivor was to take the other's share, but now Thorfinn demanded one half of the islands. Although Brusi held two-thirds of these, he was no match for Thorfinn who could get help from Scotland, so Brusi set out for Norway to ask King Olaf for assistance and he took his ten-year-old son, Rognvald, with him. King Olaf told Brusi that if he would accept his overlordship he could have his lands as a fief, for the king regarded the islands as his property, then he would give him assistance. Although Brusi objected to these terms, he had no alternative but to agree. When Thorfinn heard that Brusi had gone to see the king of Norway he decided to do likewise; the king requested Thorfinn to accept his sovereignty over the islands also, and Thorkel Fostri, who was with King Olaf at the time, having fled there after killing Earl Einar, advised Thorfinn to accept the king's demands. The king then gave Brusi one-third of the islands, Thorfinn another third and he confiscate Einar's third for the killing of Eyvind. Earl Thorfinn took his leave of the king and made his departure but Brusi stayed behind, and before he left, King Olaf gave him Einar's third also so that he would be a better match for Thorfinn. In return Brusi left his son Rognvald with King Olaf. Back in the earldom, Brusi had difficulty in contending with Vikings who were plundering the outlying parts, and he complained to Thorfinn, who wasn't doing his share of defending the islands. Thorfinn got his revenues and lived in Scotland, but he took on the defence of the whole of the earldom and was rewarded with Einar's third in addition to his own. The earldom at this time included Orkney and Shetland but later in about 1195 Shetland was confiscated by King Sverri of Norway after the islanders had supported Sigurd, a contender for the crown of Norway.

In 1016 Olaf Haraldsson, a descendant of Harald Fairhair, had seized Norway. He is said to have been baptised in Normandy, and during his reign he fought against the old heathen practices. He allied himself with his brother-in-law, the king of Sweden, against Cnut Sveynson, the king of Denmark, who is better known as Canute the Great. In 1028 Canute arrived off the Norwegian coast with a powerful fleet and Olaf fled to Russia, but he returned to Norway two years later, having crossed the mountains into the Trondelag. An army of farmers and peasants from that area of Norway led by two landowners, one being a Kalf

Arnason, defeated his small force at Stiklestad near the Trondheim Fiord. King Olaf was killed and his fifteen-year-old half-
brother Harald, who was wounded in the battle, was helped to a
lonely farmstead by Rognvald, the son of Earl Brusi of Orkney.
Rognvald then made his way to Russia where the king took him
into his service. The body of Olaf was taken to St Clement's
church in Trondheim and the Norwegian Church got a saint of
royal blood to strengthen its fortunes. Olaf's son, Magnus the
Good, built a church in Trondheim over the spot where his
father's body had lain for a night and it was called St Olaf's, and as
his fame spread throughout Europe many churches were built and
dedicated to him. Harald, the half-brother of King Olaf, travelled
to Constantinople where he became leader of the Varangians, the
Scandinavians who formed part of the army of the Byzantine
rulers. He later became King Harald Hardrada (Hard ruler) of
Norway.

Earl Thorfinn of Orkney had been given the earldom of
Caithness by his grandfather, Malcolm II of Scotland, but when
King Malcolm died in 1034, Thorfinn refused to pay tribute to the
new king for it. The new king of Scotland[4] made his sister's son,
Moddan, earl in place of Thorfinn, but Thorfinn wasn't going to
give up Caithness without a fight and he collected together a large
force. Moddan marched north to take possession of his new
earldom but was soon retreating south with Thorfinn in pursuit,
laying waste to the land. Thorfinn then returned to Caithness,
dismissed his levies and retired to Duncansby with five warships.
The Scottish king fitted out eleven warships, then sailed to look
for Thorfinn, and Moddan was sent north by land. When
Thorfinn heard of this he crossed the Pentland Firth to get help
and arrived off Deerness in the evening, but the Scottish king had
seen his sails and early the next morning Thorfinn was surprised
before any help had arrived. They fastened their ships together, as
was the custom when fighting at sea, then and the earl's scald
wrote:

---

[4] According to historians, the next king of Scotland was Duncan I, a grandson of
Malcolm II, but according to the saga he was King Karl Hundason. It has never
been discovered why the new king of Scotland was called Karl Hundason in the
saga.

Valiantly the earl went forward
'Gainst the king's eleven vessels.
Then the ships were lashed together
Know ye how the men were falling?
All their swords and boards were swimming
In the life-blood of the Scotsmen.
Hearts were sinking, bowstrings screaming
Javelins flying, spear-shafts bending,
Swords were biting, blood flowed freely,
And the earl's heart was merry.

Thorfinn's men had attacked fiercely and the Scotsmen's resistance was feeble, so Thorfinn ordered his men to board their ships and the Scots cut the ropes, took to their oars and fled back to Scotland. Thorfinn then collected a large army and went in pursuit. Moddan was now at Thurso, so Thorfinn sent Thorkel Fostri there with part of his army and Moddan was surprised at night while asleep. Thorkel set the house on fire, and when Moddan jumped out Thorkel's sword took off his head and his men surrendered. Thorkel collected men from the north of Scotland and went to join Thorfinn in Moray, then with their combined force they met the Scots. Thorfinn, wearing a gold-plated helmet, a sword in his belt and a spear in his hand, led his men and although the Scots outnumbered them again, once more the Norsemen's attack was so fierce that the Scots fled again. Thorfinn pursued them as far south as Fife, laying waste to the country as he went and then returned to Caithness where he spent the winter.

In Norway King Canute had appointed Hakon, a son of Earl Erik, as king when he forced Olaf out, but when Hakon was drowned in the Pentland Firth on his way to England, Canute made his own son, Sweyn, king. In 1035, a group of nobles brought Magnus, the son of Olaf, from Russia and proclaimed him king of Norway and Sweyn fled to Denmark. Rognvald, Brusi's son, came with Magnus to Norway, where he learned of his father's death and Magnus granted him the land in Orkney that his father, Brusi, had held and also gave him three warships. Earl Brusi had been given an extra third of the earldom, the third that belonged to Earl Einar before he was killed. King Magnus of

Norway now gave the extra third to Rognvald so that he would be a better match for Thorfinn who also held the earldom of Caithness from the Scottish king. Thorfinn needed assistance against the Irish and Hebrideans, so he allowed Rognvald to take two-thirds of the earldom if he would assist him and they became allies.

During eight summers Thorfinn and Rognvald raided in the Hebrides and in Ireland, returning home for the winters laden with plunder. They conquered much land and even invaded England, south of Man during the reign of Canute's son, Harthacnut. Kalf Arnason, who is reputed as having given King Olaf his death blow at Stiklestad, had become reconciled with Olaf's son, King Magnus, but later they fell out and Kalf was banished. He came to the Orkneys with six warships and a large following, to stay there at the expense of Thorfinn, who was married to his brother's daughter, Ingiborg. Thorfinn began to get short of provisions and thought Rognvald should be helping, so he asked for one of Rognvald's third parts of the earldom, maybe to billet some of Kalf Arnason's followers there. Rognvald refused and he sailed to Norway to see the king who had granted him the two-thirds.

King Magnus gave Rognvald all the help he required, and when he was ready he set sail and collected reinforcements first in Shetland and then in Orkney. Earl Thorfinn was in Caithness, where he lived most of the time when not on war expeditions, and news reached him there that Rognvald had arrived. Thorfinn collected his forces together and sailed for Orkney as Rognvald was crossing over to Caithness. They met off Raudabiorg, which may be the red cliffs to the east of Dunnet Head in Caithness. After some fierce fighting things began to go against Thorfinn and he cut the ropes fastening his ship and rowed for the shore with seventy dead bodies aboard. Kalf Arnason was lying nearby with six large ships, taking no part in the fighting since King Magnus had sent him word that if he assisted Rognvald he would have his estates in Norway returned to him, so he was probably uncertain which earl to support. Thorfinn, however, persuaded Kalf to assist him, and with the additional men the fight turned in Thorfinn's favour and the Norwegian levies cut themselves loose from the lashed ships and fled. Thorfinn and Kalf then attacked Rognvald's ship and he also cut himself loose. When night fell, he sailed for Norway.

Thorfinn took over all the islands and resided there, evidently in preference to Caithness. He sent Kalf to the Hebrides; Norway was out of the question since he had gone against King Magnus who had bribed him to help Rognvald. Rognvald stayed in Norway with King Magnus for a while, then requested a single ship, which was granted, and early in the winter he sailed to Shetland with a picked crew which included some of King Magnus's bodyguards or *hirdmen*. In Shetland he heard that Thorfinn was now in Orkney with few followers, so he sailed there and surprised Thorfinn at night when most of his men were asleep. After securing all the doors, the house was set on fire, which seems to have been a popular custom in those days. All his men perished in the flames, but Thorfinn, carrying his wife, leapt out unseen in the thick smoke and disappeared into the darkness. Thorfinn rowed alone over to Caithness during the night, while Rognvald, thinking that Thorfinn had died in the fire, took up residence in Kirkwall and began to prepare for the Yuletide feasting. A little while before Christmas he took a ship to Papa Stronsay to get malt for brewing, and during the evening while he and his men were sitting warming themselves at a fire in a homestead there, the house was set on fire. Thorfinn had come over from Caithness and was treating Rognvald as he had been treated himself. Rognvald repeated Thorfinn's feat by leaping clear of the men surrounding the house and disappearing into the night. Thorfinn sent search parties to look for him and he was found and slain on the beach by Thorkel Fostri when his dog barked. The next morning Thorfinn loaded Rognvald's ship with his own men and took it back to Kirkwall where an unarmed crowd of Rognvald's supporters were waiting to meet it. Thorfinn's men sprang out and slaughtered about thirty of them but one of King Magnus's hirdmen was spared to take the news to the king in Norway.

The body of Earl Rognvald was taken to Papa Westray and buried there. When King Magnus heard of the killing, he swore to avenge the deed, but at that time he was at war with Denmark.

One winter when King Magnus lay at anchor in the south of Norway, two ships were rowed into the harbour and up to the king's ship. A man wearing a white cloak boarded her and went aft where the king was sitting at a meal. He saluted the king, then broke off a piece of bread from a loaf and ate it, whereupon King Magnus offered him a drink. He then asked him who he was and the man replied, 'Thorfinn Sigurdson and I have come with two well-armed warships to offer you assistance because of the wrongs I have done you.' The king said he would consider the matter and they often met for the king's ships were at anchor there for a long while. One day when they were both sitting drinking together, one of the king's hirdmen, the one whose life Thorfinn had spared in Kirkwall, came up to them and asked Thorfinn what compensation he was going to pay for the killing of his fellow hirdmen in Kirkwall. Thorfinn replied that he was not in the habit of paying compensation for men he killed, and when he saw that the king's anger was roused Thorfinn returned to his own ship.

The next morning the king's fleet sailed south to Jutland and Thorfinn returned to Orkney. That summer King Magnus, who is given the name 'Magnus the Good', fell ill and died and his uncle Harald Hardrada, who the king had named as his successor and who had now returned from his adventures in the east, became king. In about AD 1050 Thorfinn set out on a pilgrimage to Rome to obtain absolution for all the sins he had committed. He went to Norway first and was well received by the new king; he then sailed to Denmark where he was entertained by King Sweyn, then overland to Saxony to be guest of Emperor Henry III. The emperor gave him many horses and he rode south to Rome. On his return Earl Thorfinn built Christ Kirk in Birsay and here the first bishop's see in the Orkneys was established; when Thorfinn died in 1064 he was buried there.

Thorfinn's sons, Paul and Erlend, succeeded to the earldom and the saga says that Paul, the eldest, ruled for them both. Paul married a granddaughter of Magnus the Good of Norway and this was to be the cause of trouble between their sons Hakon and Magnus later.

Edward the Confessor, king of England, died in 1066. He had no heir and Harold, son of Earl Godwin of Wessex, who was

Edward's brother-in-law and one of the most powerful men in England at that time, claimed that on his death bed the king had named him as his successor and he was crowned king shortly afterwards. His brother Tostig, who had lost his earldom of Northumberland, was in exile on the continent, and as he wished to regain his lost earldom he went to Norway to see King Harald Hardrada, who was a great warrior, to invite him to invade England. Harald agreed and towards the end of 1066 a great invasion fleet sailed to the northern isles, where King Harald collected a large force and the earls Paul and Erlend. The fleet then sailed south before a northerly wind, the same wind that was keeping the invasion fleet of William, Duke of Normandy, bottled up in a harbour on the French side of the English Channel, for he was also bent on invading England. Edward the Confessor's mother was Emma, a daughter of Richard I of Normandy, from whom Duke William was descended, and it has been said that as Edward of England had a liking for the Normans he may have promised William the kingdom of England since he had no heir. When Duke William heard that Harold had been crowned king, he immediately gathered his followers together but his fleet was delayed by the unfavourable weather.

Harald Hardrada, King of Norway, landed on the English coast near Scarborough and set the town on fire before sailing up the Humber and defeating two English earls. He then marched towards York; the town surrendered and a meeting was arranged with the town's officials for the next day. During the night Harold Godwinson arrived at York with a large army and sent a message to his brother, Tostig, who had by then joined Harald Hardrada, saying that he could have his earldom of Northumberland back if he withdrew his troops. Tostig asked the messenger what the king of Norway would get. 'Seven feet of earth for a grave,' replied the messenger and they then prepared for the Battle of Stamford Bridge in which both the king of Norway and Tostig fell. The victorious Harold Godwinson allowed Harald Hardrada's son, Olaf, and the two earls of Orkney to return to their homes with the remnants of the Norwegian army.

By now Duke William had landed in England, and when Harold Godwinson got this news he hurried south to deal with him, but was defeated at Hastings on 14 October 1066, an event and date well known in history, and Duke William was crowned king of England.

After returning from Stamford Bridge, Paul and Erlend ruled together for a while, but when their sons grew up they caused dissension between the earls. Paul's son, Hakon, regarded Erlend's son, Magnus, as his inferior because of his mother's royal blood. Their councillors tried to reconcile the two earls, but Erlend refused to co-operate if Hakon remained in the islands, so he was persuaded to go abroad for a while. Hakon went to Norway and then to Sweden where his mother's relatives were, and there was peace and quiet in the islands again.

In Norway, Magnus Barelegs was now king and he decided to make an expedition to the Western Isles of Scotland. He was called Barelegs because he discarded his trousers for a kilt or skirt. He sailed with a fleet of sixty warships and took with him his eight-year-old son Sigurd whom he set up as earl of Orkney after sending Paul and Erlend into exile to Norway. He then sailed to the Western Isles and caused much devastation there before sailing further south to Wales.

When the men were preparing for a battle in the Menai Strait, Magnus, the son of Earl Erlend of Orkney who was accompanying the king on this expedition, refused to arm himself, then sat down and sang from a psalter while the fighting went on about him. To escape the king's anger he slipped overboard at night, swam ashore and made his way to the Scottish court. After the battle the victorious King Magnus turned north towards Scotland and the Scottish king sent messengers asking for peace and offering Magnus the Western Isles which he took possession of before sailing home in the following spring. When he reached Orkney he learnt that the two Orkney earls had died in Norway, so he arranged a marriage between Gunnhild, the daughter of Earl Erlend, and Kol, the son of Kali, one of his favourite warriors who had died of wounds received during the battle in the Menai Strait.

After King Magnus's death a few years later in Ireland, Hakon, son of Earl Paul, got his half of the earldom from the king's sons. Magnus then returned to Orkney to claim his share; Hakon told him to get acknowledgement from the kings of Norway, so

Magnus sailed there and was invested as earl. For a few years the two earls agreed and went on war expeditions together until their old quarrels broke out. When they were on the verge of conflict, the councillors or leading men again saved the situation. They arranged a meeting between the two parties on the isle of Egilsay during Easter week. Magnus was the first to arrive at the island and when he saw the number of Hakon's ships approaching, he realised that he could expect treason and went into a church on the island to pray. In the morning, Hakon, sword in his hand, went in search of Magnus who he found at prayer in a refuge and, being resigned to his fate, Magnus refused to allow his men take up arms on his behalf.

Magnus reminded his cousin of the oaths he had taken, and to save him committing a further sin by shedding blood Magnus suggested that he be allowed to go to Rome and obtain absolution for them both. He promised never to return to Orkney. This plea was turned down, so Magnus suggested that he be sent to Scotland and kept in close confinement. This was also rejected. Magnus's third suggestion, that he be maimed and thrown into a dark dungeon, was agreed to by Hakon, but his chiefs told him that one of them must die for if there were two earls there would never be peace, to which Hakon replied, 'Slay him, for I would rather have the earldom than death.'

Magnus was slain with an axe there on the island of Egilsay. His mother, Thora, was permitted by Earl Hakon to give her son a Christian burial and his remains were taken to Christ Kirk in Birsay. Soon after it became a place of pilgrimage and illnesses were miraculously cured at Magnus's grave.

After Magnus's death, Hakon took possession of the whole earldom and a few years later he visited Rome and Jerusalem. After this pilgrimage he lived a more peaceful life and he probably built the round church at Orphir. He introduced better laws for the bonders or landowners and he became popular; by the time he died his former misdeeds were almost forgotten.

Hakon's two sons, Paul II and Harald I, were half-brothers and they divided the earldom between themselves, but they didn't agree. Harald held Caithness from the king of Scots and sometimes resided there, as did his mother Helga, daughter of Moddan of Dale in Caithness. Harald went to the islands and with his men slew Thorkel, the son of Sumarlidi, a great friend of Earl Paul. Paul banished those who took part in the crime and Harald paid compensation for the killing, as was the custom. In an attempt to keep the two earls on friendly terms they were persuaded to spend the main festivals together, and one Christmas Paul was being entertained by Harald at his hall in Orphir. Harald's mother, Helga, and her sister, Frakok, the widow of a Sutherland chieftain, were staying with him at the time and Helga planned the murder of Paul so that her son could get the whole earldom, but fortunately for Paul the scheme went amiss.

The saga says that Helga and Frakok were preparing a fine linen shirt as a present for Paul. The shirt was embroidered with gold, but impregnated with poison, and Harald, Paul's half-brother, found the shirt and after putting it on was seized with a great trembling and had to be carried to his bed, where in a short while he died in great pain. Maybe this episode, like the shirt, was embroidered to enhance it, but nevertheless, Harald was poisoned in error. The two scheming sisters left the islands, while Paul with the consent of the bonders took possession of Harald's half of the earldom.

Kol, who had married Gunnhild, the sister of Earl Magnus, resided in Norway, while his son Kali was brought up there. In 1129 King Sigurd of Norway, who had himself been earl of Orkney some years previously, granted Kali the half of the islands that had belonged to Magnus. Kali's name was changed to Rognvald for luck and he became very accomplished, as the following verse which he wrote bears out:

> At the game-board I am skilful,
> Knowing in no less than nine arts,
> Runic lore I well remember,
> Books I like, with tools I'm handy,
> Expert am I on the snow-shoes,
> With the bow and pull an oar well
> And besides, I am adept,
> At the harp and making verses.

Before Rognvald claimed the earldom King Sigurd died and his son Magnus didn't renew the title, but when Harald Gilli, an illegitimate son of Magnus Barelegs, became king, he confirmed the grant. In 1135 Rognvald's father, Kol, sent envoys to the Orkneys to ask Earl Paul to give up a half of the islands to Rognvald; if Paul refused the messengers were instructed to proceed south into Caithness and offer Frakok, daughter of Moddan of Dale, half of the earldom if she would take it by force. Paul refused, so the messengers as instructed went on to Caithness and Frakok told them that it was a wise decision to seek her assistance. She told them to return to Norway and tell Rognvald that she would have a force ready by the middle of the following summer to do battle with Paul. The family of Moddan of Dale had claims to the earldom and Frakok's sister, Helga, the mother of the poisoned Earl Harald, had a daughter, Margaret, married to the Scottish earl of Atholl and another married to the king of the Hebrides, so they had many friends to assist them.

In Norway during the winter Rognvald set about preparing his invasion force and in the summer he sailed to Shetland. Earl Paul heard of the arrival of Rognvald's ships when he was in Rousay staying with his friend Sigurd of Westness, so he mobilised his forces and his chiefs arrived in five warships. Frakok and her grandson, Olvir Rosta, had collected twelve vessels in the Hebrides and these under the command of Olvir sailed for Orkney in the summer, as Frakok had promised. Paul got warning that Frakok's fleet was approaching from the west and he decided to engage it first before sailing for Shetland to deal with Rognvald. As he passed Tankerness, Olvir rounded the Mull Head of Deerness so Paul lashed his ships together and took on board stones for ammunition. Olvir's ships approached and there was some fierce fighting in which Olaf Rolfson of Gairsay cleared three of Olvir's ships. Olvir boarded the earl's ship and, leading his men in the attack, hurled a spear at the earl who caught it on his shield. Sweyn Breastrope, Earl Paul's henchman, picked up a large stone and threw it at Olvir with such force that it knocked him overboard unconscious. He was dragged aboard one of his own ships and his men cut their ropes and fled. When Olvir came to, he tried to persuade his men to return to the fight, but the earl's ships were now in pursuit and Olvir was chased past South

Ronaldsay into the Pentland Firth. Five of Olvir's ships were captured and Paul manned these with his own men and with his enlarged fleet sailed for Shetland.

Paul reached the Shetlands unexpected and found Rognvald's ships lying in Yell Sound waiting for a favourable wind to sail south. Rognvald and his men were ashore being entertained by the Shetlanders so Paul slew the men on watch aboard the ships and took possession of them. In the morning Rognvald was told that his ships had been captured and he went down to the beach and challenged Paul to come ashore and fight, but Paul was wary of the Shetlanders and sailed back to Orkney. Rognvald and his men remained in Shetland until the autumn when they returned to Norway aboard merchant ships.

Paul kept on the alert so long as Rognvald was in Shetland; he had a warning beacon built on Fair Isle which was to be lit if ships were seen coming from Shetland. The warning would then be passed via a similar beacon on North Ronaldsay and by other beacons in the Orkney group. When Paul heard that Rognvald had left Shetland he relaxed and prepared a grand Yule feast at his Orphir estate. Just before Yule, Olaf Rolfson of Gairsay, who was the earl's deputy in Caithness, was at his homestead in Duncansby when Frakok's grandson, Olvir, made a surprise attack. Sweyn, Olaf's son, was luckily fishing in the Pentland Firth with the sons of Grim of Swona and when he returned home he discovered that the homestead had been surrounded by Olvir's men and the house set on fire with Olaf inside. Sweyn, Olaf's son, and his two friends rowed over to Orkney, where Sweyn was invited to be a guest of Earl Paul.

The earl's drinking hall at Orphir had a door in the southern wall that led to a magnificent church. This will be the round church thought to have been built by Earl Hakon. At this church the guests attended the Yule services then returned to the hall for drinking sessions. After his father's death, Sweyn, Olaf's son, became known as Sweyn Asliefsson, Aslief being his mother's name. At one of the drinking sessions he was seated in the hall next to Sweyn Breastrope, the earl's henchman, who called him a sluggard at drinking his ale, and before the night was out Sweyn was provoked by a kinsman into killing Sweyn Breastrope.

Eyvind, his kinsman, gave Sweyn an axe and as they were on their way to mass at the church the earl's henchman was struck down. Sweyn Asliefsson, accompanied by Eyvind's son, left the hall and rode in the dark by a path between the hills to the Bay of Firth, where they found a boat and crossed over to Damsay. Sweyn got in touch with Bishop William who was pleased when he heard the story, for Sweyn Breastrope was disliked by the bishop because he practised sorcery. The bishop sent Sweyn to the isle of Tiree in the Hebrides, where he stayed throughout the winter and Earl Paul outlawed him.

In Norway Kol persuaded his son Rognvald to have another attempt at winning the earldom, and Rognvald assembled an invasion fleet. While waiting among the islands off Bergen for a suitable wind, Rognvald made a speech to his men saying that he intended to win the Orkneys or die. His father then stood up and said that it was his wish that if Rognvald should win the earldom he should make a vow to build a magnificent stone minster at Kirkwall, dedicate it to his uncle Magnus who had been murdered by Hakon, endow it with money and make it the seat of the bishops of Orkney. The vow was made and, accompanied by his father, Rognvald sailed west for the Shetlands when the wind became favourable.

On Fair Isle, Paul had a warning beacon and Kol devised a plan to deceive the watchers there into thinking that an invasion fleet had sailed. He left Shetland on a course for Orkney with a fleet of small boats. When they were in sight of Fair Isle he ordered his men to row backwards to reduce speed. The sails were then set and gradually raised, which gave the illusion of a fleet approaching. The beacon on Fair Isle was lit and when Kol saw this he ordered his ships back to Shetland, while the warning was passed on by the beacon on North Ronaldsay and other Orkney beacons. Paul assembled his forces and waited on the alert for three days before it was realised that it had been a false alarm. Kol then sent a Norwegian who lived in Shetland to Fair Isle with a tale that he had been robbed by Rognvald's men. He took a house there and when he got an opportunity he poured water over the warning beacon so that when Rognvald sailed the beacon was too wet to be lit. Rognvald sailed to Westray in Orkney and the Westray men submitted and swore oaths of allegiance.

Early in the spring Sweyn Asliefsson left the Hebrides and went to stay for a while with Countess Margaret and Earl Maddad of Atholl. Countess Margaret was Earl Paul's half-sister and, besides being very beautiful, was also very ambitious. Sweyn and Margaret had secret consultations together, and shortly afterwards Sweyn sailed to Thurso where he fitted out a ship with a crew of thirty men, then sailed across the Pentland Firth. He found out that Earl Paul was staying in Rousay with the chieftain Sigurd of Westness, and Sweyn sailed up Evie Sound to Rousay. Here he discovered Paul otter-hunting near Scabra Head so he landed with his men and killed the earl's followers and dragged Paul aboard his ship. When the otter-hunting party failed to turn up for their morning ale, Sigurd sent men to look for them and the slaughtered men were found but there was no sign of Paul. Sweyn, with his captive, sailed past the cliffs of West Mainland and into Hoy Sound, took the channel between Hoy and Graemsay and then into the Pentland Firth by Hoxa Sound. Paul was taken to Countess Margaret in Atholl and nothing was ever heard of him again. Maybe he was put to death, but whatever happened Countess Margaret sent Sweyn back to the Orkneys to let it be known that Paul would never return, and when the Orkneymen heard this they submitted to Rognvald as Paul's successor.

Soon after this, in about 1137, the foundations of St Magnus Cathedral were laid. Red sandstone for building the cathedral was quarried at the Head of Holland about three miles east of Kirkwall and Rognvald's father, Kol, who had remained in Orkney to supervise the building, sent ships to England for masons. Before long the funds were exhausted, and after consulting his father Rognvald took possession of all the odal land. He then announced that the landowners could redeem their land on payment of a sum of money depending on the amount of land they possessed, which brought in sufficient funds to continue the building.

In 1138 the Bishop of Atholl arrived in Orkney and after being entertained by the earl and bishop of Orkney, he explained that Paul had been kidnapped so that Harald, the five-year-old son of Countess Margaret of Atholl, could be made earl in his place. The removal of Paul had made it easy for Rognvald to take over the earldom and after a meeting of the earl's councillors, it was agreed that Harald should be given the title of earl and have a half of the earldom. When Harald arrived in Orkney he was accompanied by Thorbiorn Clerk, a grandson of Frakok, who married a sister of Sweyn Asliefsson while in the islands, and Thorbiorn became Sweyn's friend for a time. Sweyn was now allowed to take over his father's estates and he became a great chieftain. In Gairsay he had a large drinking hall where he and his men would gather when not away sea roving. In the spring the seed had to be sown, while in the autumn it had to be harvested, so summer was the time that any business was attended to. One year Sweyn decided that it was time to avenge his father's death and after getting two ships from Earl Rognvald, he sailed to the Moray Firth. He then went overland to Sutherland and took Olvir Rosta by surprise, killing many of his men, but Olvir himself escaped to the mountains and is heard of no more in the sagas. Sweyn plundered the homestead, then set fire to the houses, burning Olvir's grandmother, Frakok, and the other inmates inside. He then ravaged and plundered in Sutherland and further south before going back to Orkney. The next summer Sweyn returned to the Hebrides after hearing that his old host in Tiree was having his estates plundered by Welsh raiders. He went to Wales where he burnt and plundered many homesteads and returned with much booty; in the winter he married Ingrid, the wealthy widow of a chieftain of the Isle of Man who had been killed by the Welsh pirates. Sweyn had been married before so this was his second marriage, and after a time he sold his newly acquired estates and returned to Gairsay in Orkney with his new wife.

Sweyn's next expedition was back to the Hebrides, where he plundered and burnt far and wide, killing many people, and he returned with his ships loaded with booty. He caused enmity on his return when he demanded a large share of the booty because he was the leader, and as they were at Duncansby his demand was agreed to for he had numerous followers in that part of Caithness. The ships had been supplied by Earl Rognvald again, and Thorbiorn Clerk, who was captain of one of the ships, went to

Orkney and complained to Earl Rognvald, then he divorced his wife who was Sweyn's sister and Sweyn considered this a great insult.

When Sweyn wasn't at his estate in Duncansby, an old acquaintance, Margad, a son of Grim of Swona, looked after his affairs there. Margad murdered a Norwegian living in Wick, who was a friend of Earl Rognvald, and the son of the murdered man asked Earl Rognvald to help him avenge the killing of his father. Earl Rognvald crossed over to Caithness accompanied by Thorbiorn Clerk and two others who had been cheated out of their proper share of the plunder after their return from the Hebrides. Sweyn and Margad took refuge in a stronghold known as Lambaborg which was situated on a high crag, transversed by a strong wall to protect it from attack by land. Lambaborg has been identified as the Broch of Ness, south of the Freswick burn. Rognvald found Sweyn at Lambaborg and demanded that Margad be handed over, which Sweyn refused to do. Rognvald decided on a siege and as Sweyn had sixty men to feed the provisions were soon exhausted and it was realised that they would have to surrender. In the dark Sweyn and Margad were lowered down into the sea on ropes and they then swam south and came ashore where the cliffs ended. In the morning the garrison surrendered. The drenched fugitives made their way to Moray where they came across a trading vessel manned by an Orkney crew in which they sailed to the Isle of May in the Firth of Forth. They were detained here by bad weather and while there Sweyn plundered the monastery on the island. They then visited David, the king of Scots, in Edinburgh who thought highly of Sweyn and he made up the losses suffered by the monastery that Sweyn had pillaged. Sweyn told the king that he wished to become Earl Rognvald's friend again and the king sent an embassy to the Orkneys with presents and a message requesting the earl to make peace with Sweyn. This Rognvald promised to do and Sweyn returned to his estate in Gairsay, while Margad remained with the king.

About this time King Ingi, son of Harald Gilli, invited Earl Rognvald to visit his court at Bergen in Norway and he immediately accepted the invitation for he had many friends and kinsmen there. Harald Gilli claimed to be a son of Magnus Barelegs and a

Celtic mother, a native of the Hebrides. Rognvald and Harald Gilli, King Ingi's father, had become friends when they met in Grimsby when Rognvald, then Kali, had been there on a trading trip. The teenage Harald Maddadson, the son of Countess Margaret of Atholl, asked to be allowed to accompany Rognvald and in the spring the two earls sailed for Bergen with some merchants. They spent most of the summer in Norway and while there Rognvald became acquainted with an Eindridi Ungi who had just returned from Constantinople where he had probably been a mercenary in the emperor's bodyguard, the Varangians. He persuaded Rognvald to lead an expedition to Jerusalem; they were to have two winters to prepare and no one except the earl was to have a longship of more than thirty benches.

King Ingi gave Rognvald two small longships and in the autumn they left Bergen and sailed to the west, Rognvald in a ship called *Hjalp* and Harald in one called *Fifa*. The next day there was a great storm and in the dim light they saw land ahead so, with breakers everywhere about them, they ran the vessels ashore on to a narrow stony beach beneath some cliffs near Gulberwick in the south of Shetland. There was no loss of life and the Shetlanders were glad to see the earl and he stayed for a while before sailing for the Orkneys.

During Yule, the Christmas festival, Earl Rognvald entertained Bishop William who agreed to go on the crusade as an interpreter and a number of the chiefs promised to accompany the earl. After the two winters had passed, Rognvald returned to Bergen to see the ship that was being built for him in Norway. It was a magnificent carved and gilded ship with thirty-five benches and when the expedition was ready it sailed for Orkney. As it was now autumn it was decided to winter in the Orkneys, during which time there was much quarrelling between the Norwegians and the Orkneymen. This will be when the Maeshowe burial chamber was broken into, for one of the runic inscriptions on the walls of this chamber states that Orkahowe was broken into by 'Jerusalemfarers' in search of treasure, Orkahowe being the Norse name for the Maeshowe burial mound. Early the following year, Rognvald arranged a meeting with the chiefs who weren't sailing with him to tell them that he was leaving the government of the islands in the hands of his kinsman Earl Harald, who by then was about twenty years old, and he requested them to obey him. The expedition of fifteen large ships left in the summer and sailed through the English Channel to Spain, and after a number of adventures on the way it reached Jerusalem. At this period the Holy Land was in the hands of the Crusaders and the earl bathed in the Jordan. After visiting Constantinople, they sailed to Italy where the earl and the bishop and a number of the nobler men left their ships to visit Rome, from where they rode overland back to Norway.

While Rognvald was away, events were happening in the Orkneys. Shortly after Earl Rognvald left, a King Eystein of Norway, who was on his way to plunder in England and Scotland, for some reason seized Earl Harald in Thurso and held him as a prisoner until he paid the king a ransom for his release and swore fealty to him for Orkney and Shetland. Later that same year, Erlend, son of Harald I, arrived in Orkney to claim a share of the earldom. He had been given the title of earl with one half of Caithness by the young King Malcolm of Scotland. With a strong force he crossed over to Orkney to claim half of the islands. Harald Maddadson, who had been left in charge of the islands by Rognvald before he sailed for the Holy Land, refused to give up half of the islands, but before there was any bloodshed Erlend went to Norway to see King Eystein, who apparently was opposed to Earl Harald for he gave his half of the earldom to Erlend. At this time Sweyn Asliefsson had a disagreement with Harald who, having been left in charge by Earl Rognvald, had apparently exiled Sweyn's brother, Gunni, when Countess Margaret of Atholl, widow of Harald's father, went to Orkney and had a child by Gunni. Sweyn sent Gunni to the Hebrides and when Erlend came to the Orkneys from Norway, Sweyn joined forces with him and advised him to make Harald give up the islands immediately. They found Harald aboard his ship and, after a fight, with many wounded on both sides, the island's chiefs intervened between the two parties and Harald agreed to give up the islands.

For two months Erlend and Sweyn ruled the islands and then during the Yule holiday Earl Harald made an unsuccessful attempt to surprise Erlend. He crossed over the Pentland Firth, but was delayed at Orkahaug where two of the party were seized by madness. When Rognvald arrived back in Orkney he made an agreement with Erlend that they should share the earldom and defend it against Harald, then Rognvald went over to Caithness. He was in Sutherland at the wedding of his daughter when Harald who had been in Norway came to Caithness. Rognvald's daughter had married an Erik Slagbrellir who was related to Harald and he tried to make peace between the two earls. It was arranged for them to meet at Thurso and here some of Harald's followers attacked Rognvald's men, killing thirteen of them, but they were then separated and peace was restored. The two earls were urged by many of those present to renew their old alliance, which they pledged to do and they shook hands and decided to attack Erlend that night. After crossing the Pentland Firth in ten ships they went ashore in Orkney, but Sweyn and Erlend had been warned by spies. Sweyn decided to go to Caithness where he took a large number of cattle aboard his ship, and let it be known that they intended to go to the Hebrides for the winter.

Sweyn and Erlend left Thurso with six longships and took a course westward, with the crews rowing. When they came to the Point of Stoer on the west coast of Scotland, Sweyn ordered his men to turn the ships about and set the sails. The men thought this was foolish, but he had kept his plan from them, and with a favourable wind they retraced their course and made for Walls on the island of Hoy. Here they heard that Rognvald and Harald had thirteen ships lying at Scapa, which was a larger force that Sweyn had, so he decided to surprise them by attacking at night. It was getting near to the Yule festival again, and one night during a shower of sleet, Earl Rognvald and six of his men left their ships to go to the earl's residence at Orphir. Sweyn's strategy had succeeded so well that Rognvald wasn't expecting any trouble. They spent the night at Knarston near Scapa, where an Icelander called Botolf lived, and while Rognvald slept there, Erlend and Sweyn attacked the ships lying at Scapa, taking Earl Harald by surprise. Some of Erlend's men looking for Rognvald called at Knarston and Botolf deceived them into thinking that he had gone to a nearby hill, where they rushed off to, hoping to be the first to catch him. Botolf then woke Rognvald and he escaped to the earl's residence at Orphir where he found Harald in hiding, and they both crossed over to Caithness. Sweyn sent Rognvald's property which was found in his captured ship over to him, and advised Erlend to move to Walls so that he could keep a lookout for an attack from across the Pentland Firth; but as it was near Yule, Erlend was persuaded by his men to go to Damsay in the Bay of Firth where they could feast and drink at the castle.

Just before Christmas, Sweyn had to go to a kinswoman of his called Sigrid, who lived in Deerness, and while he was away Rognvald and Harald crossed over from Caithness to make a surprise attack. Erlend, who was aboard his ship lying off the island of Damsay, was dead drunk at the time, and two days later his body was found among seaweed on the shore of Damsay with a spear shaft sticking out of it.[5] Most of the earl's men had also been drunk at the time of the attack and were killed, but those who escaped took refuge in St Magnus Church in Kirkwall. The Earls Rognvald and Harald went to St Magnus Church, which is how the cathedral is named in the saga, and Erlend's men who were there all swore fealty to them.

After Erlend's death, Sweyn went to Rendall where a kinsman lived and found out all about what had happened. He took his ships to Rousay where he beached them and with five men he crossed over to the other side of the island to a farmstead where some of the earls' men were. In the darkness they hid themselves outside the building and here they heard one of the men boasting of having given Erlend the death blow. When they heard this, Sweyn and his men burst in, and Sweyn struck dead Erlend's killer. Rognvald now wanted to make peace with Sweyn so he sent a message which invited Sweyn to spend Yule with him. Sweyn accepted the invitation and after Christmas a meeting was arranged between Sweyn and the two earls so that they could try to come to a settlement. Some of those present at the meeting wished Sweyn to be exiled from the islands as he was always causing trouble but they agreed to a proposal that he should be allowed to keep half of his estate in Gairsay and one good longship.

---

[5] There is a stone in St Magnus Cathedral in Kirkwall which bears the name of Erlend, so it will probably be the gravestone of this earl.

Rognvald wouldn't accept any money from Sweyn, but Earl Harald went to Gairsay and used Sweyn's grain and other possessions. When Sweyn heard of this he considered it a breach of their agreement and went to his homestead in Gairsay with ten men, but Harald wasn't there. Some of his men were and they surrendered, so Sweyn took their weapons and let them go free, then poured out all the beer and took his wife Ingrid and their daughter away with him. Harald had gone hunting hares on some other island, and when his men told him about what had happened, he went in search of Sweyn and found him with a few followers in a small boat and pursued him. The saga says that Sweyn went to Hellisey,[6] an island that rises abruptly from the sea, and which has a large cave in the cliffs, the mouth of which flooded at high tide. When Sweyn realised that Harald was in pursuit, he made for this cave, hauled his boat up into it and the tide rose and closed the entrance. During the day Earl Harald and his men searched Hellisey in vain for Sweyn and concluded that he must have left the island.

Sweyn took a ship belonging to the monks and went to Sanday and then to South Ronaldsay. Early one morning, Sweyn and his men saw a large longship coming to South Ronaldsay and Sweyn recognised it as Earl Rognvald's ship for he had commanded it himself. After a show of aggression by Sweyn, they agreed to talk, and while they were talking Earl Harald's ship was seen sailing from Caithness to Walls. Sweyn asked what was to be done and Rognvald advised him to go to Caithness, but while on his way there Earl Harald saw the ship and thought he recognised it as Sweyn's, so went in pursuit. Sweyn landed on Stroma, an island in the Pentland Firth, and Harald took his ship there. A man called Amundi, who lived on Stroma, was acquainted with both the earl and Sweyn and he succeeded in making peace between them. The next morning, Sweyn went on to Caithness, while Harald went to Orkney and then to Shetland. After Easter Sweyn returned to Orkney and met Earl Rognvald at Birsay, while at Whitsun Harald

---

[6] Early scholars took this island to be Helliar Holm off Shapinsay, but it is now thought more likely to be Eynhallow, an island situated in the middle of a swift tide race between the island of Rousay and the Evie coast off the main island of Orkney.

arrived from Shetland and they held a meeting of peace in St Magnus Church in Kirkwall. Earl Harald returned to Sweyn a longship that had belonged to him and Sweyn went on a plundering expedition to the Hebrides soon afterwards.

During the late summer it was the custom for the earls to go hunting deer in Caithness and when Rognvald had been earl for about twenty-two winters, the two earls went over to Caithness. Going up Calderdale, a valley near Thurso, Rognvald was riding at the head of his men with two companions when they came to a homestead where the farmer, a man named Hoskuld, was working on top of a corn stack. Thorbiorn Clerk, Earl Harald's former councillor who had been outlawed by Rognvald for killing one of his men, was inside the farmhouse drinking, and Hoskuld greeted Rognvald by name in a loud voice as he approached. This could have been a pre-arranged signal, for when Thorbiorn heard the greeting, he and his men seized their weapons and ran out of the house into a narrow passageway which was probably between the farm buildings. Thorbiorn struck at Earl Rognvald from a wall which would have been more level with Rognvald who was mounted, but as he dismounted Rognvald's foot stuck in the stirrup and he was struck again and mortally wounded. Thorbiorn and his men ran down a steep bank at the rear of the homestead, which stood on high ground. When Earl Harald arrived, Earl Rognvald's men were standing around the dead body of their earl and they urged Harald to go after Thorbiorn. By now Thorbiorn and his men were on the other side of a marshy bog and the two parties found themselves facing each other on opposite sides. Thorbiorn pleaded with Harald for mercy, saying that it had been Rognvald's intention to kill him, and he reminded Harald that he had been Rognvald's servant, but now he would have control of the whole earldom. Magnus Gunnisson, one of Harald's men, spoke up, saying that if Harald didn't avenge the killing, Rognvald's followers would think that he had been implicated in it, and Magnus and a few who agreed with him made their way around the bog.

Realising that no quarter could be given, Harald leapt across the bog in full armour, maybe mounted on his horse, and his men tried to follow; they didn't make the far bank, however, and fell in the mud and had to pull themselves out. Thorbiorn now decided to speak to Harald, who told him to save himself, so he and his followers made their way to a deserted shieling which Magnus Gunnisson set on fire, and when Thorbiorn and his men came out they were slaughtered. There is no evidence that Harald was implicated in the murder of Rognvald and his reluctance to give proper justice to Thorbiorn Clerk could have been because Thorbiorn had been his foster father when he was young. The saga says that Harald brought the body of Earl Rognvald to the Orkneys and that it was buried in the Magnus Kirk.

After Rognvald's death, Harald took possession of all the islands and he became friends with Sweyn again. Sweyn took Harald's son, Hakon, with him on his marauding expeditions, and on one of these Sweyn is given the credit of killing the great Hebridean chief, Somerled. According to Scottish history, however, Somerled was killed at the Battle of Renfrew while fighting against King Malcolm of Scotland. When Sweyn wasn't sea roving he was at his home in Gairsay, a small island with a cone-shaped hill, which can be seen from the road between Evie and Finstown. At Langskaill in Gairsay, Sweyn had the largest drinking hall in Orkney and just below the house there is said to be an ancient pier made from huge blocks of stone. Near the pier is a long narrow building, the foundations of which are thought to be those of Sweyn's drinking hall, where in 1171 he entertained Earl Harald. While there, Harald suggested to Sweyn that he should stop his sea roving before he lost his life and Sweyn replied that he would make his autumn cruise his last as he was getting old. After the seed was sown he went on his spring cruise and came home for the harvest and then went off on his autumn cruise. This autumn cruise of 1171 proved to be, as he had said, his last.

With seven longships Sweyn sailed to Ireland and attacked Dublin. The town surrendered and he and his men returned to their ships, but on the following day, as they returned to the town of Dublin to receive a payment of money, the Norsemen fell into pits which had been dug during the night. Sweyn was slain and so passes out of the saga one of Orkney's greatest Viking sea rovers.

At this period Norway had many kings, probably because

descendants of past kings seized the throne from the one who had previously claimed it. In 1163 a Magnus Erlingson, who claimed to be a descendant of Sigurd the Crusader, was crowned at Bergen. In 1184 King Magnus Erlingson was slain by Sverri, who claimed to be a descendant of Harald Fairhair. Ten years later a party of Norwegians who were championing Sigurd, the son of Magnus Erlingson, asked Earl Harald of Orkney for help and the earl gave permission for any chieftain to join the Norwegians if he wished to do so. Most of Sigurd's supporters were either from Orkney or Shetland and at first they had some success, but then, in the spring of 1194, Sverri suddenly attacked them when they were lying in Floruvoe, near Bergen. The islemen dragged their ships together to make a fighting platform, but in their hurry most of the oars were broken, a misfortune that proved to be fatal for them. King Sverri had smaller ships than the islemen and he kept attacking and withdrawing, then he withdrew all his ships. The islemen cut their lashings to give chase and found out too late that they had no oars; then each ship was attacked individually by Sverri, and Sigurd and all his supporters who didn't surrender were slain.

The next summer Earl Harald, the bishop and all the chief men of Orkney accompanied Harald to Bergen where he pleaded with King Sverri and prostrated himself before him and was pardoned. The estates of all the islemen who had been slain at Floruvoe were confiscated with the condition that they would be redeemed with money in three years' time, otherwise they would become the property of the king of Norway. Shetland, with its skat and other taxes, was confiscated and it became the property of the king of Norway, who placed his own bailiff there and also encouraged the use of a lawman, a royal official who gave legal advice at the things, meetings where matters concerning peace in the islands were settled.

The saga says that Earl Harald Maddadson was a great chief. He divorced his first wife, Afrika, a sister of the earl of Fife, and married Gormflaith, daughter of Malcolm MacHeth of Moray. The MacHeths of Moray had been contenders for the Scottish crown but by now Gormflaith was the only living survivor. Earl Harald was a son of Earl Maddad of Atholl in Scotland and he held Caithness from the Scottish king, who granted a half of Caithness to a grandson of Earl Rognvald, who was known as Harald Ungi, meaning Harald the Younger, a name given to him to distinguish him from the older Harald Maddadson. Harald Maddadson refused to give up a half of Caithness, and when Harald Ungi asked for half of the earldom of Orkney which had been granted to him by the king of Norway, Harald Maddadson crossed over to Caithness where Harald Ungi was and slew him in a battle. This was in 1196 and today an edifice called Harald's Tower stands on a hill near Thurso which is claimed to have been built on the spot where Harald Ungi lost his life.

The north of Scotland was a troublesome region for the king to control, and when he heard of the aggressive actions of Harald Maddadson, he asked Rognvald, king of the Hebrides, a descendant of Earl Hakon of Orkney, to take possession of Caithness. This he did, and after being there a while he returned to the Hebrides, leaving behind stewards to administer the territory. Earl Harald had remained quietly in Orkney when these events were taking place, but now he considered it time to act so he sent an assassin to murder the stewards and was successful in getting rid of one of them. Harald then sailed to Thurso and anchored in Scrabster Roads and when he landed he was met by the bishop of Caithness who resided nearby. The bishop, who wished to save the people of Thurso from any unnecessary trouble, pleaded with the earl on their behalf, but the earl was in a bad temper and he is also said to have had a grudge against the bishop for refusing to collect a papal contribution of one penny from every household in Caithness that Harald had granted to the Church with the approval of the pope in Rome. The earl had the bishop's tongue cut out and he hanged the principal inhabitants who opposed him and imprisoned those who couldn't pay a heavy fine that he imposed on them. Earl Harald stayed in Caithness while the remaining stewards who had escaped being murdered fled south to tell the king of Scotland what had happened.

The king of Scotland was furious at this further outrage against his authority and he collected a large army from all parts of his kingdom and marched north. He camped his troops in the valleys between Caithness and Sutherland; when Harald learned off the size of the king's army he begged for terms and the king, with undeserved leniency, granted a pardon. The king demanded a large sum of money for the return of Caithness to Harald, who consulted the men of Caithness and they agreed to pay the fine, and peace was restored again. Earl Harald Maddadson lived a few more years after getting back Caithness and died in 1206. The earl's eldest son, Thorfinn, had been taken as a hostage by the king to ensure the future good behaviour of the earl, but when the earl continued to aggravate him, the king had Thorfinn blinded. His other sons, John and David, succeeded him and ruled together until 1214 when David died, and then John became sole earl.

The bishop of Caithness was now a Bishop Adam, who is said to have taken advice from a monk called Serlo. Probably through the bishop being badly advised by the monk, the bishop's skat, which was paid in butter, was increased to such an extent that the populace rose in revolt. In the year 1222 Earl John was residing at Brawl Castle, the episcopal manor at Halkirk. On a hill near the castle an annual fair was being held, at which many of the local people were gathered, and they went to see the earl to complain about the injustice of the tax. The earl didn't want to interfere even though he disapproved of the unfair tax, but being annoyed at the persistence of the complainers he is reputed as having said, 'The devil take the bishop, you may roast him if you please.' And the crowd of local people, taking this as being authorised by the earl, set off for the bishop's palace. The bishop and Rafn, a lawman, were sitting in an upper room at the time, drinking ale and discussing the subject of the tax, and the lawman advised the bishop to drop his demand for an increase. Through a window they saw an unruly mob and heard shouts of 'Roast him alive!' Realising that things were getting serious, the lawman and the bishop sent Serlo the monk out to investigate, but when he made an appearance he was felled to the ground and then trampled to death. The lawman went out and said that the bishop was disposed to reduce the tax, but when the bishop appeared in his robes of office he was stripped and dragged to the kitchen and burnt in the fire. Those who took part in the killing were severely punished by the king who was commended by Rome for the action.

In 1224 Earl John was summoned to Norway by the king who suspected him of being implicated in an uprising in Norway. When he returned to Orkney he had to leave his son Harald behind as a hostage and Harald was drowned in 1226, probably on his way home after being released.

The next event of note was a Norse expedition to the Western Isles in about 1230. The Norse influence in the Western Isles had been weakened during the twelfth century when the Scottish chieftain Somerled of Argyll defeated Godfrey, the Norwegian king of the Hebrides, and took part of his kingdom from him. The Norse influence must have continued to weaken, for the expedition of 1230, or thereabouts, is said to have been in support of the tottering Norse dominions in the west.

At this time there lived in Orkney a young man called Snaekoll Gunnason whose father had married Ragnhild, the granddaughter of Earl Rognvald. Snaekoll claimed Rognvald's private estates, which the earl refused to give up, and as usual it ended in a state of enmity between the two parties. In the year 1231 Snaekoll and a friend, Hanef Ungi, a commissioner appointed by the king of Norway to collect his revenues in Orkney, were drinking in a tavern in Thurso when a man ran in and told them that the earl was staying at an inn in the town. They grabbed their weapons and rushed to the tavern and the earl ran down into a cellar where he was found and slain. As soon as they had sobered up, they returned to Orkney and went to the island of Wyre where they drove a herd of cattle into the castle there for provisions, then settled down to await an attack. Friends of the late earl sailed to Wyre and besieged the castle, but as it was strongly built it withstood the siege and to end the deadlock kinsmen came and arranged a truce, the terms being that both parties should go to Norway the next summer and have the king of Norway act as arbitrator. The next spring two ships sailed for Norway, one containing nearly all the kinsmen of the late earl, while the other transported Snaekoll and his friends. When they arrived in Norway, some of Snaekoll's party were slain by the late Earl John's kinsmen. It is recorded in Icelandic annals for the year 1232 that kinsmen of Earl John were lost at sea. This is presumably when they were on their way back to Orkney.

The Hereditary Scottish Earls

Earl John is called the last of the Norse earls, but his father Earl Harald Maddadson was a son of the Scottish Earl Maddad of Atholl, who was descended from the ruling house of Scotland, and this is probably why Earl Harald wasn't frightened to defy the king of Scotland at times. Henry, a son of Harald Maddadson by his first wife Afrika, a daughter or sister of an earl of Fife, is said to have become earl of Ross. The earldom of Ross had been created by the king out of the eastern part of Moray, so that he could get some control over that troublesome region. Harald Maddadson was also being troublesome at that time and the king took part of the earldom of Caithness from him. Malcolm MacHeth of Moray, the father of Gormflaith, the second wife of Harald Maddadson, had revolted against the king and after his death chroniclers say that Gormflaith persuaded her husband to occupy her father's territory. It was for this reason, it is said, that the king took possession of the part of the earldom of Caithness known to the Norsemen as 'the south land' and made it into a new earldom of Sutherland. This was given to William Freskin, a son of the sheriff of Inverness, in about the year 1230.

The earls of Orkney were also earls of Caithness, which they held from the Scottish king, but after 1230 they would have only held a half of it. An heiress, Joan of Strathnaver, who married Freskin of Duffus in Moray, inherited a share of the remainder of Caithness, so only a small portion would have been left for the Scottish earls of Orkney to inherit. Magnus II, probably the son of an earl of Angus, is usually named as the first of the Scottish earls of Orkney after the Norse period, although Harald Maddadson was the son of a Scottish earl, but he continued on in the manner of the Norse earls. Magnus II, who was probably descended through his mother from an Orkney earl, died in about the year 1239 and the Orkney earldom then passed to a Gilbride or Gilbert who also belonged to the Angus family.

Magnus III, probably a son of Gilbert, succeeded Magnus II and a little more is known about him than about the former Angus earls of Orkney. In 1263 he sailed from Bergen for Orkney in a longship given to him by Hakon Hakonson, the then king of Norway. During the thirteenth century Bergen became the capital of Norway and King Hakon built a hall there with a large chamber on an upper floor which he used on ceremonial occasions. This hall was damaged during the last war but has been restored since and the impressive large chamber was later used for a series of world conferences. In the same year that Magnus III returned to Orkney, King Hakon sailed from Norway with a great fleet, bound for the west of Scotland. The king's ship was built with oak and had a gilded dragon's head at its stem and it lay with other Norwegian warships in Orkney before sailing to disaster and defeat.

Hakon of Norway was showing Alexander III of Scotland that he was prepared to defend the Western Isles of Scotland which, like Orkney, had been settled by the Norse and which the Scottish king now wanted to add to Scotland. It was the time of the autumn gales and while sheltering off the west coast of Scotland some of King Hakon's ships were blown ashore. When the Norwegians landed, they were overcome by the Scots. What remained of the Norwegian fleet returned to Orkney with a sick king who took up residence with the bishop of Orkney in Kirkwall and he died there towards the end of the year. King Hakon lay in state in the upper hall of the Bishop's Palace for two days clad in noble robes and then the remains of the great king were interred in the cathedral until spring when the king's ship conveyed them to their final resting place in the choir of Christ's Church in Bergen, Norway. When King Hakon sailed for the west coast of Scotland, Earl Magnus was expected to follow, probably in the longship Hakon had given him, but there is no evidence that he ever did. His loyalty would have been divided between the Norwegian and Scottish kings and had he sailed he would have been disloyal to the Scottish king, while if he didn't he would have been disloyal to the king of Norway. He seems to have chosen to go to Scotland and may have never returned to Orkney.

Hakon's son, Magnus VI, persuaded the Norwegian assembly that the Western Isles, being so remote, were of little value to Norway, and in 1266, at the Treaty of Perth, they were ceded to Scotland together with the isle of Man for the sum of four thousand merks sterling[1] plus an annual rent of one hundred merks sterling. Payments were to be made in the country of Orkney at certain specified dates, but over the years Scotland defaulted on the payments, so to keep the two countries on friendly terms a wedding was arranged between Margaret, the daughter and heir of Alexander III of Scotland, and Eric, the oldest son of Magnus VI of Norway. They were married in 1281, but Margaret died two years later leaving a daughter, Margaret, the 'Maid of Norway', who was chosen as heiress of the Scottish throne at a parliament held at Scone in February 1284. On the death of Alexander III in 1286, after being thrown from his horse, she became queen of Scots and Edward I of England arranged a marriage between his eldest son and Margaret. During September 1290 she sailed from Norway, but unfortunately the eight-year-old princess died in Orkney in the arms of the bishop of Bergen, either because of seasickness or through the ship being wreaked in the islands and this upset Edward I's plans. Had the Maid of Norway survived, Scottish history may have been different. There may have been no war of independence, for Edward I of England promised that Scotland would keep her independence. Some Scots, however, such as Wallace and Bruce, if the marriage had taken place, may not have trusted Edward I to keep his promise.

Before the birth of Alexander III, Robert Bruce, Lord of Annandale, had in 1238 been named as successor to Alexander II, as he was a grandson of David, earl of Huntingdon, the king's uncle. As Scotland was again without an heir he claimed the throne along with other contestants while Edward I of England demanded that these contestants for the throne of Scotland should accept him as their overlord. In June 1291 he summoned the Guardians and other magnates of Scotland to Norham on the Tweed to swear fealty to him, and in the following year, at a court hold at Berwick, John Balliol was selected by Edward I as the next

---

[1] One merk sterling is considered to have had a value of two-thirds of a pound sterling or thirteen shillings and four pence.

king of Scotland and he was crowned at Scone.

In 1294 Edward I declared war on France, and as the new Scottish king had agreed to Edward I being his overlord, Edward I demanded military help from Scotland. John Balliol was little more than a puppet king under Edward I, so a Scottish parliament elected a council of four earls, four barons and four bishops to be responsible for affairs of state. This council of twelve Guardians made an alliance with France, which angered Edward I, and in March 1296 he marched over the border to punish the Scots. He massacred the citizens of Berwick along with the city garrison, and defeated a Scottish army at Dunbar. He then marched to Scone from where he removed the coronation seat of the Scottish kings, the Stone of Destiny, and sent it south to Westminster Abbey. Balliol surrendered to Edward I, and was sent to England and later allowed to retire to France where he died.

When Balliol was in exile, patriotic Scots fought for his cause, the most outstanding being William Wallace who joined forces with Andrew Murray and defeated an English army at Stirling Bridge in 1297. The Scottish spearmen assembled on the south-facing slopes of Abbey Craig[2] about a mile north of a narrow bridge across the River Forth at Stirling. When part of the English army had crossed the bridge, the Scots attacked and seized the north end of the bridge, which trapped those who had crossed, and the English on the south side looked on helpless as their comrades on the other side of the river were massacred by the Scots. Stirling Bridge was a decisive victory for Wallace and Murray, but in the following year Wallace was defeated at Falkirk by an army led by Edward I in person.

Robert Bruce, earl of Carrick, a grandson of Robert Bruce of Annandale, was also fighting for Scottish independence, and in 1306 was crowned king of Scots at Scone in defiance of Edward I of England, but in the same year he was defeated by an English army. This was at Methven near Perth, and Robert Bruce then disappeared from the mainland of Scotland for four and a half months. Magnus V, earl of Orkney, was Scottish and supported Bruce for he was one of the eight earls whose seals are attached to

---

[2] Perched on top of Abbey Craig is the Wallace Monument which was built in about 1865.

the Declaration of Arbroath. This was a document sent to Pope John XXII at Avignon in 1320 requesting him to recognise Bruce as king of an independent Scotland. Bruce's sister was the widow of the deceased King Eric of Norway and lived in Bergen so he had connections with Norway and Orkney. After Methven, Bruce's wife and daughter were taken prisoner by the English at Tain and were presumed to be on their way to Orkney where one of Bruce's supporters, the bishop of Moray, had taken refuge. Bruce was known to have been at Dunaverty Castle in Kintyre before he disappeared from the mainland of Scotland and, evading English ships which were patrolling the west coast, it is thought that he took refuge either in Northern Ireland or the Hebrides. There is, however, a piece of tradition concerning a knight in armour who crossed the Pentland Firth on the day of the Battle of Bannockburn, who is taken as being St Magnus of Orkney, which must strengthen any belief that there was some connection between Bruce and the islands.

When Bruce returned to the mainland of Scotland in 1307 via the isle of Arran he was more successful and by the beginning of 1314 most of the castles had been captured from the English. Stirling Castle was besieged by his brother Edward and the English commander promised to surrender the castle on 14 June if he wasn't relieved by then. Edward I was now dead, but his son Edward II took up the challenge and gathered together a large army and marched over the border. He arrived at Stirling to find Bruce barring his approach from the south. Some English cavalry men who attempted to reach the castle by making a detour to the north of Bruce's position were routed and turned back. Edward decided to camp for the night, as they were now near enough to relieve the castle on 14 June, the following day. The English army crossed the Bannock Burn and made camp in the Carse of Stirling, a marshy area between the higher ground of New Park where Bruce's army was encamped and the Forth. They were better equipped and had a larger army than the Scots, and Bruce thought that it might be wiser to retreat to the hills, so he consulted his commanders, and it was decided to surprise the English by attacking in the morning. The English camp was among the pows, the sluggish burns that ran into the Bannock

Burn, and it was here that the battle of Bannockburn took place. The large English force was unable to manoeuvre and was trapped in the marshy ground where they had spent the night. It turned into a massacre, with Edward II luckily escaping to Berwick.

On the death of Magnus V some time after 1320, the Angus line of Orkney and Caithness earls came to an end, and these earldoms passed by marriage to the Scottish earls of Strathearn. During the troubled times following Bruce's death, the earl of Strathearn lost Strathearn and a Malise of Strathearn moved north to Brawl Castle in Caithness, which was probably the seat of the Strathearn line of earls of Caithness. Malise will be a Celtic or possibly a Pictish name because the district of Strathearn, together with Menteith, formed the Pictish province of Fortriu. Although twice married, this Malise had no male heir, but had a number of daughters. An early document states that his eldest daughter, Matilda, was married to a Weland de Ard.

On Malise's death in about 1344, Alexander, a son of Weland de Ard, under the laws of Scotland, inherited Caithness, while in 1353 a Swedish noble, Erngils Suneson, who had married another daughter of Malise, was given the title of earl of Orkney by King Magnus of Norway and Sweden. Another daughter of Malise married a Guttorm Sperra who was also a Swedish noble. The male line of the Norwegian kings had ended in 1319 when Hakon V of Norway died, and as a daughter of Hakon had married a son of the Swedish king, their son Magnus became heir to the throne of Norway, and he was also elected to be king of Sweden. In 1357 King Magnus took the title of earl of Orkney from Erngils Suneson because he sided with a party of Swedish nobles who supported a contestant for the throne of Sweden.

In 1362 King Magnus's son, Hakon, married Margaret, a daughter of Waldemar, king of Denmark, and Henry Sinclair of Roslin in Midlothian was present at this wedding which took place in Copenhagen. He probably went there as a representative or ambassador of Scotland, but he undoubtedly had another reason for going. When the earldom of Orkney became vacant on the death of Earl Malise, his descendants are stated as having intrigued to get possession of it, and while in Copenhagen Henry Sinclair, whose mother is assumed to have been another daughter of Malise, had his name put forward as a claimant. His uncle Thomas was appointed Norwegian bailie or agent for Orkney and he began his duties by distributing positions of importance to his friends and relatives. By 1369, however, Thomas was replaced by a Hakon Jonsson and in that year an agreement was made in Kirkwall between Hakon, the new Norwegian bailie, and the bishop of Orkney, who was a Scotsman. In this agreement the bishop consented to take more native men of Orkney and Shetland into his service, so, like Thomas, the bishop was employing Scotsmen in preference to the native inhabitants.

In 1375 Alexander de Ard was appointed to govern the islands for a period of one year, but as this appointment was then terminated he is considered to have been unsuitable. In the same year that he was appointed governor of the islands, Alexander de Ard handed over Brawl Castle in Caithness to Robert II of Scotland, and he also resigned the rights to land he had inherited there. When in 1263 Hakon of Norway sailed to the Western Isles, Magnus III was placed in an awkward position because he held Orkney from the Norwegian king and Caithness from the Scottish king and would have wondered which king to support. Maybe Alexander de Ard was trying to placate the Norwegian king by giving up his Scottish inheritance, but if this was the case he was unlucky for he was unsuccessful with Orkney. This divided loyalty, however, didn't deter King Hakon VI of Norway from granting the earldom to Henry Sinclair of Roslin a few years later.

In 1379 Henry Sinclair was invested as earl of Orkney by King Hakon VI. Over the years the islands had deteriorated into a state of disorder because for some time there had been no one with much authority in the islands except the bishop, and he didn't get on very well with the king of Norway or the inhabitants. At Henry Sinclair's investiture as earl, he had to promise the king of Norway 'not to establish any union or make friendship with the bishop, but to assist the king against him until he should do what is considered right by the king'. Earl Henry also promised not to tolerate any interference from his cousins, Alexander de Ard and Malise Sperra. In the year 1382 Bishop William of Orkney is recorded as having been slain. Malise Sperra, the son of one of the daughters of Earl Malise, resigned his rights to the earldom, but in spite of this he was slain after a dispute concerning land at the althing, the supreme court of Shetland over which Earl Henry was presiding as chief magistrate.

During Norse times, after the king of Norway defeated an uprising of the islesmen of Orkney and Shetland at Floruvoe, near Bergen, Shetland was taken from the earls of Orkney and for nearly two hundred years Shetland was ruled by a foude who was appointed by the king of Norway and later by the king of Denmark. The foude performed the duty of chief magistrate at the althing, an annual event held at Tingwall, at which disputes were settled. The althing was also a social occasion at which the odallers, owners of land, and probably their families also, attended and met friends from all parts of the islands. The court at Tingwall is said to have taken place on a small islet in Loch Tingwall, where the foude and his officials sat on stone seats in the open, but the islet is now a promontory, for since that time the level of the water in the loch has fallen.

During Norse times the Shetland Islands were divided into districts where smaller foudes acted as magistrates at smaller district courts, called things. These courts occurred more frequently than the annual althing and matters left unsettled at the thing were taken to the annual althing at Tingwall. During the later Norse period the chief magistrate had a residence in Scalloway which is a few miles south of Tingwall. At this time Scalloway was the capital of Shetland and when an althing was to take place, huts were put up for accommodation there and it is probably from these that Scalloway got its name, skali being old Norse for a hut. When Earl Henry Sinclair became earl of Orkney he was also given Shetland to govern, and as he evidently acted as chief magistrate at the althing he could have had a residence in Scalloway as the chief magistrate had in the later Norse period. Scalloway could have then been the main landing place for ships coming from Orkney, there being a good harbour there, although it would be more exposed to the Atlantic than a harbour on the east side of Shetland. Lerwick, on the east side of Shetland, grew in importance during the seventeenth century and took over the role of capital.

In 1520 some pieces of old letters found in Venice told of how a Venetian sea captain accompanied by a person called Zichmni had crossed the Atlantic to the North American continent in 1398. It has been thought that the letters were some sort of hoax, but others consider them to be genuine. According to the letters, the sea captain Nicolo Zeno was sailing his ship up the English Channel when it was caught in a storm and driven northwards. It was wrecked on an island called Frislanda which belonged to Zichmni, who is presumed to be Earl Henry of Orkney. The captain and the crew were rescued by Zichmni, who was at Frislanda at the time, and he gave the captain the command of one of his ships. In return the captain taught Zichmni new techniques in building warships, for the Venetians were reputed to be an authority on naval matters at this time. Frislanda is taken as being Fair Island, a part of Shetland which was under the control of Earl Henry and where a ship of the Spanish Armada, the *El Gran Grifon*, was also wrecked. The letters are called the Zeno letters as they belonged to the Zeno family, a sea-going Venetian family. A sea chart probably drawn to illustrate the narrative is not very accurate for the islands are placed in the wrong position, including Frislanda which is in the middle of the Atlantic. The narrative was compiled from pieces of old letters and with the sketchy information it would be difficult to decide if the story was genuine.

Before the date of the alleged Zeno voyage[3] across the Atlantic, an overland caravan route to and from the east had come to an end. The Venetians had done a lot of trading with eastern countries, and like Christopher Columbus one hundred years later, they may have hoped to find a western route to the riches of the east. The caravan route known as the Silk Road started from Sian in China, the city of the terracotta soldiers and now Edinburgh's twin city. It crossed deserts and mountains to markets at Acre and Tyre on the Mediterranean coast and during crusader times Venetian merchants traded at these markets. They also traded with Arabs for spices brought by Arab dhows from the Moluccas or Spice Islands and a large part of the spices used by Europe passed through Venice. At the beginning of the fourteenth century Marco Polo, the son of a merchant of Venice, had

---

[3] The Zeno voyage to America is included in *Divers Voyages Touching the Discovery of America* by Richard Hakluyt, 1582.

travelled extensively in the east, while his father had taken the Silk Road to China, but shortly after this time, the Silk Road was abandoned because of a change of circumstances in the Far East. The Khans from Mongolia had conquered China in the thirteenth century but in 1368, however, the Chinese pushed the Mongols back into the steppes of northern Asia and the Ming dynasty of China started. The Mings closed the country to foreigners and the overland trading routes fell into disuse.

The Zenos were a leading seafaring family of Venice. When the Genoese were defeated at the naval battle of Chioggia in 1381, a relative of Nicolo Zeno, Carlos Zeno, had been in command of the Venetian fleet while Nicolo had command of a warship. Earl Henry is known to have sailed to Greenland in about 1398 so maybe he was persuaded to explore further west, but if he did so no record of such a voyage exists.

There had been a Norse settlement in Greenland since the time of Erik the Red, who arrived there at the end of the tenth century, and there had been a bishop at Gardar in an eastern settlement since 1126. There was also a western settlement which was found to be deserted in about 1350, the reason being unknown. In 1394 there was still a bishop at Gardar for in that year Bishop Henry of Orkney was ordered by the pope to exchange his diocese with that of Bishop John of Gardar, but during the next century the eastern settlement also came to an end, the reason for which could have been a deterioration of the weather.

The existence of Greenland was known in Orkney during the time of Earl Thorfinn because of ships being driven there by storms, and when Erik the Red was outlawed from Iceland he sailed there and after exploring the area he brought colonists from Iceland. He himself settled at a farm called Brattalid which was on a fiord that bears his name, Eriksfiord, which was in the eastern settlement. During his time an Icelander called Biarni Herjolfson sailed to join the settlers in Greenland, but was blown off course and arrived at an unknown land to the west. When he eventually reached Greenland he told of this new land he had seen and Leif Eriksson, a son of Erik the Red, bought his boat and sailed to find it. He arrived at a land where there was trees and an abundance of grapevines, so Leif called it Vinland, and after loading his ship with timber, which was a scarce commodity in Greenland, he sailed home. According to the sagas, four shiploads of Norse colonists later sailed for Vinland and settled there, but after conflict with the native inhabitants they eventually decided to leave. The place where these colonists settled is thought to have been in the island of Newfoundland, where in 1961 a Norwegian author and explorer, Helge Ingstad, excavated a site at Epaves Bay on the northern tip of the island and claimed that it contained evidence of Norse occupation in about the year 1000.

Earl Henry built a castle in Kirkwall which was at the sea's edge, as the bishop's castle seems to have been. The entrance to Henry's castle was in the wall facing Bridge Street, in which direction a wooden bridge sloped down to a lower level. In 1615 rebels holding the castle dismantled this wooden structure, which made it impossible for the attackers to reach the entrance, it being well above ground level. Dirleton Castle in East Lothian, the home of the wife of Earl Henry, is entered in a similar manner, over a wooden bridge to an entrance high up in a wall, so this could have been the custom at that time of constructing an entrance to a castle. The walls of Kirkwall Castle were over ten feet thick and they withstood the bombardment of cannon brought from Scotland by the earl of Caithness, but after the rebels surrendered he had it destroyed and the ruins remained until removed in 1865 when Castle Street was built. A large plaque is fixed on the gable end of number one Bridge Street to commemorate the castle, which was actually sited across the end of Castle Street. An area near the cathedral is known as Castle Yards, but the only visible remains are a defaced and weather-worn heraldic stone above the plaque that commemorates the castle; this bears a coat of arms showing in one quarter the remains of a galley shaped like the horns of a cow or ox. This heraldic stone is stated to have been over the entrance to the castle.

Henry's father, after surviving the plague of 1350, was killed while fighting alongside fellow Scots on the continent; Earl Henry was killed in about the year 1400 while defending Orkney from invaders. He is recorded as having married Janet, a daughter of Sir Thomas Halyburton of Dirleton, a small picturesque village in

East Lothian, by which marriage he had a son, Henry, who succeeded him as earl of Orkney.

It is considered that Henry II probably didn't spend much of his time in Orkney so would have resided mostly at his castle of Roslin in Midlothian, maybe getting the produce of the islands shipped there to stock up his larder. This was a time of unrest on the border between England and Scotland and during a battle at Humbledon Hill in Northumberland it is stated that Earl Henry II was taken prisoner by the English. He must have been released before 1406, for in that year he was again taken prisoner by the English, while accompanying Prince James of Scotland to France.

Robert III of Scotland was weak and enfeebled and his eldest son, David, had been starved to death in Falkland Castle by the duke of Albany, so he arranged for his second son, James, to be sent to France for safety, and it was probably in his capacity as admiral of Scotland that Earl Henry accompanied the prince. They sailed from the royal burgh of North Berwick in 1406, probably passing between the Bass Rock and the then newly built Tantallon Castle on a headland opposite to it. This could have been the last sight of Scotland that the prince had for eighteen years, for on their way to France they fell into the hands of the English and were taken as prisoners to the court of Henry IV. Shortly after hearing of this, Robert III died, and his son, the prince, remained a captive in England until 1424. Earl Henry was imprisoned in the Tower, but is said to have escaped and reached Scotland safely. In about 1420 Earl Henry II died of a serious illness. He married a daughter of Sir William Douglas of Nithsdale in Dumfriesshire, by which marriage he received the lordship of Nithsdale and the office of custodian of the Marches.

After the death of Henry II the administration of the islands was entrusted by King Eric of Denmark to Thomas Tulloch, the newly inducted bishop of Orkney. Before he died Earl Henry appointed his brother-in-law, David Menzies of Weem, to look after his affairs in Orkney, and after a visit to the Danish court in 1423 Menzies became governor. For seven months he plundered the country in the style of the later Stewart earls, until the people complained to Denmark and Menzies was removed and sent to England as a hostage. When Prince James was released from captivity, hostages were sent to England until a large ransom was paid.

After Menzies was removed, the Orkney people declared unanimously that they would have no governor other than William, the earl's heir, and in 1434 he was installed with his followers promising him resolute allegiance. King Eric of Denmark had rejected William's claim through the lack of convincing documented proof, and it wasn't until after a document known as 'The Diploma to the Succession of the Earldom of Orkney' was prepared by Bishop Tulloch that the king of Denmark acknowledged his right to the earldom. This document gave particulars of William's descent from the first earl, and the reason given for there being no documented proof of this was that the principal house of the earls had many times been burnt and plundered by invaders and any charters and papers had been burnt, destroyed or taken away. This could be the reason why, if Henry I did go on a voyage west of Greenland, there is no record of it. Henry I was killed by invaders in about 1400 and in 1460 raiders were still invading the islands: for a letter sent in that year to the king of Denmark to explain why the earl hadn't appeared at the Danish court stated that MacDonald, Lord of the Isles, had continuously, year by year, sent raiders to burn, plunder and kill the inhabitants of the islands.

In 1435, probably as hereditary admiral for Scotland, Earl William sailed to France with Princess Margaret, the eldest daughter of James I, and in the following year she married the dauphin, thus strengthening the Scottish-French alliance. In 1437 King James, an unpopular king, was slain by nobles who were tired of the heavy taxation imposed on them to pay for the king's ransom when he was released from captivity in England and resented his abandonment of the Scottish hostages.

In about 1455 his son James II took the inherited Douglas lordship of Nithsdale together with the office of sheriff of Dumfries and warden of the Marches from Earl William and gave him the earldom of Caithness in compensation.

During the reign of James I all the old agreements between Scotland and Norway regarding the Western Isles and the Isle of Man made at the Treaty of Perth in 1266 had been renewed, but the annual payments had evidently lapsed again for during the reign of James II, Christian I, the king of Denmark, Norway and Sweden, being short of money because of wars, demanded payment of the arrears. As Scotland couldn't raise the money required, it was suggested at a conference held in France in 1460 that, in order to keep the two countries on friendly terms, James, the son of James II, should marry Margaret, the daughter of Christian I, but later that year James II was killed at the siege of Roxburgh Castle when one of his own guns accidentally exploded and the marriage proposal was put to one side. In 1468 a mission which included Bishop William of Orkney was sent from Scotland to Copenhagen where a marriage contract was prepared and signed.

At the 1460 conference, when the marriage was first suggested, the Scottish ambassadors had asked for the return of the Orkney and Shetland Islands as they had belonged to Scotland before the Norse took them over. They still belonged to Norway for they were not included in the Treaty of Perth and they now became pawns in the dowry business because Christian I was short of money as Scotland was when asked to pay the arrears of the treaty's annual payments. The Danish king ruled Norway at this time, and as the islands belonged to Norway and not Denmark he may have been reluctant to hand them over as a wedding gift in case of Norwegian protests, if the Norwegians were in a position to do so, for the Norwegian parliament is stated to have been composed mainly of Danish members at this time. However, as Scotland wanted them and Christian I was short of money he must have come to the decision to hand over, as it states in the marriage document, 'our lands of the isles of Orkney' as a security until fifty thousand florins of the dowry could be paid to the king of Scotland. Under this arrangement Norway couldn't call the islands a total loss, for Christian I had retained the option of buying them back, which he may have thought would be more acceptable to any Norwegian who might feel like protesting. The dowry had been fixed at sixty thousand florins of the Rhine, plus the gift of the annual rent of one hundred merks sterling due to Norway for the Hebrides and Man, and Christian I also cancelled the arrears of the annual rent of the Treaty of Perth which had accumulated over the years. The Danish king promised to pay the remaining ten thousand florins of the dowry to the mission before it returned to Scotland, but he found he couldn't raise that amount of money so he included 'our lands of the isles of Shetland' as a security for eight thousand florins, hoping to find the balance of two thousand florins, but this may never have been paid.

During July 1469 the sixteen-year-old princess, accompanied by a train of Danish nobles and the Scottish ambassadors, landed at Leith and soon afterwards the marriage took place in the Abbey Church of Holyrood in Edinburgh.

In 1455 the Scottish parliament had passed an act which decreed that in future crown lands were to be of two categories: annexed lands and unannexed lands. The annexed lands were to be untransferable and were to be retained for the use of the crown, while the unannexed lands could be disposed of at the king's pleasure. The unannexed lands would have been granted to someone for the service of a knight or some small tribute to remind the person that the king was his overlord. The Scottish parliament would have been conforming with this act when it annexed the earldom of Orkney and lordship of Shetland in 1472.

In 1584, owing to the increasing expenses of the crown, another act of parliament was passed which ruled that all land coming to the crown was to be annexed, and only granted on feu ferme tenure. In 1504 Parliament had given authority to the king to grant feu ferme charters for all crown land. This meant that it was to be held on heritable tenure and the tenant had to make a payment for being granted it and pay feu duties yearly.

In 1472 the earldom of Orkney and lordship of Shetland were annexed to the Scottish crown by an act of parliament which stated that they were not to be given away to anyone except one of the king's sons by lawful marriage. They were never given away to a lawful son of any king of Scotland, but Robert Stewart, an illegitimate son of James V, got them from his half-sister, Mary Queen of Scots. There were a number of annexations after the Stewarts were deposed, while after the rebellion of 1745 estates were forfeited and the land annexed, so it was apparently the normal procedure for parliament to annex land when it became property of the crown.

Soon after the wedding, Earl William had to hand over Orkney and Shetland. He has been said to have lost them for an offence against James III of Scotland, but he was given Ravenscraig Castle in Fife and some land in exchange, so it may have been some sort of business deal. The earldom had been hereditary since Norse times and Earl William had been appointed by the king of Denmark. James III appointed himself earl of Orkney, so he was acting as if he had complete control over the islands and not just as if he had them temporarily until they were redeemed. This might confirm, as has been stated, that Christian I renounced his claim on Orkney and Shetland when his grandson James IV was born, although this has been disputed. Later kings of Denmark are said to have tried to get them back and in 1668 Denmark's right to redeem the islands was recognised at Breda in the Low Countries by an assembly of European diplomats, but it is thought not to be very likely that Denmark would now want to, considering today's prices.

Although Earl William lost Orkney and Shetland, he still had Caithness. This had been granted to him in 1455, in compensation for the lands of Nithsdale in Scotland, which had been acquired for the crown. Earl William of Orkney was buried in a church that he had founded and dedicated to St Matthew, but he had died before it was completed. His son abandoned the plan and finished off what had been built with a wall and the jagged stonework here is evidence of where the work on the church ceased. It is situated near the castle of Roslin in Midlothian and is known as Rosslyn Chapel, in which the tombstone of Earl William is. The chapel was built by architects and masons brought over from the continent and has a vaulted roof and ornamental pillars, and is now a tourist attraction.

During a tour of Scotland in 1803, Dorothy, sister of the poet William Wordsworth, visited Roslin and wrote in her diary: 'Roslin Castle stands upon a woody bank above a stream, the North Esk... I never passed through a more pleasant dell than the glen of Roslin. The banks are rocky on either side and hung with pine woods...' From the chapel a path leads down to the ruins of the castle of which only the west wall and a sixteenth-century block with a corbelled turret and numerous dungeons beneath remain. At the entrance to the dungeons is a seven-hundred-year-old yew tree, older than the castle itself, while in the walls here are dents that could have been made by cannon balls. The castle was bombarded by the English in 1545 and during the time of Cromwell when one of the walls was battered down.

Earl William's titles, it was said, would weary a Spaniard, and among them he is said to have had the 'Knight of the Cockle', given to him by the king of France. Earl William was first married to a daughter of Archibald, earl of Douglas, a granddaughter of Robert III of Scotland, and by her he had a son, Lord William of Ravenscraig, and a daughter, Katherine, who married the duke of Albany. By a second marriage to a daughter of Alexander Suther-land of Dunbeath, he had Sir Oliver of Roslin and William, who succeeded him as earl of Caithness and who was killed at the Battle of Flodden in 1513. A descendant of Lord William made a short stay in Kirkwall while fleeing to the continent after the 1715 uprising. He saw the remains of the castle and, being disgruntled, wrote that the family had brought ruin on itself by serving the Stewarts and that Earl William had lost the earldom for the offence of protecting and defending the king's brother, the duke of Albany, who was married to the earl's daughter. The duke of Albany had conspired with some of the nobles to dethrone his brother, James III, who caught and imprisoned him in Edinburgh Castle. He made a daring escape from the castle, which may be worth relating.

Friends of the duke of Albany arranged to have two wine kegs delivered to his dungeon. One contained the wine while the other a coil of rope with a note urging him to escape. The duke invited the captain of the guard with three of his men to sup with him and sample the wine. The duke's servant plied them with food and wine and by the end of the evening the four guests were helplessly drunk. The duke stabbed them to death with the captain's dagger, then threw the four bodies into the fire which blazed in a fireplace that must have rivalled those in the earl's palace in Kirkwall. After letting themselves out with the captain's key, the servant was lowered down with the rope over projecting rocks, but the rope proved to be too short and, risking injury, he dropped on to the rocks below, breaking his thigh. The duke lengthened the rope with bedclothes and climbed down without mishap, then carried his injured servant to Leith where a French wine lugger was waiting in the roads to take them to safety.

In France the duke of Albany married a daughter of the earl of Boulogne, after having divorced Earl William's daughter. A few years later he was back in Scotland with his lands restored, but when he started to intrigue again to gain the crown he had to flee back to France where he died.

The Stewart Earls

James III was now earl of Orkney, although there is said to be no record of his ever having used this title. As earl he would have received the earldom skat, which was a tax to cover the defence of the islands, and he would have had a large portion of the land, but not land that was bishopric or privately owned land such as that inherited by the odallers. About this time the bishopric was transferred from the see of St Nidaros in Norway to that of St Andrews in Scotland and the archbishop of St Andrews was sent to Rome to get the pope's approval of the dowry transaction.

In a charter of 1486, James III of Scotland granted Kirkwall the status of a royal burgh of Scotland. He must have decided that the king of Denmark would be unable to scrape together sufficient money to redeem the islands. James's charter also gave St Magnus Cathedral and certain local land to the burgh of Kirkwall and also gave permission to erect a tollbooth and a Mercat Cross, to hold a market once a week and a fair once a year. From the time of this charter Kirkwall was governed by a provost, four bailies and fifteen councillors and the population as well as the trade increased. Being a burgh of Scotland, the crown would have collected taxes from the merchants for trading and, being a sea port, export duty also.

King James III died in 1488, slain near Stirling, after a group of defiant nobles had seized his teenage son. He had been disliked by some of the nobles, but his son James IV was popular and Scotland began to prosper. James III had leased the crown and earldom lands to the bishops, but in 1489 Lord Henry Sinclair of Ravenscraig was given the lease with the office of justice and the custody of Kirkwall Castle. He was seldom in Orkney himself so his brother William Sinclair of Warsetter in Sanday represented him. As a noble of Scotland, Lord Henry would have had certain obligations, and when in 1513 James IV decided to invade England as a diversion to aid King Louis of France, Lord Henry fell with the king and most of the nobility of Scotland at the Battle of Flodden. After Lord Henry's death his widow, Margaret Hepburn, was granted her husband's lease, while his brother, William of Warsetter, was given his office of justice. After William of Warsetter's death, Lord Henry's son, William, through his mother's influence, it is said, was appointed justice depute of Orkney, but his stay in Orkney came to a sudden end two years later when James and Edward, sons of the late William of Warsetter, attacked and captured Kirkwall Castle with a party of armed followers. The young Lord William was forced to leave Orkney, and the next year a messenger who arrived from Scotland commanding the rebels to surrender up the castle was thrown into prison. With the royal request ignored, the earl of Caithness was instructed to put down the rebellion and with a force of about five hundred men landed on the Orphir coast of the Orkney mainland during 1529.

The Orcadians met the Caithness men at Summerdale, in Stenness, to fight for their independence. Their weapons appear to have been pitchforks for they are said to have thrown these down and showered the invaders with stones so successfully that the invasion was turned into a rout. The Caithness men were slaughtered as they fled to their boats, the earl slain at a nearby farm when trying to evade his pursuers, and Lord William was taken prisoner.

Six years later James Sinclair of Brecks, the leader of the rebellion, was knighted, given the office of justice and granted the islands of Sanday and Stronsay. The reason for this generosity could have been a policy of appeasement by the Scottish crown as James of Brecks may have been the most suitable person to control the islands, or maybe in case James of Brecks and the king of Denmark collaborated to throw off the Scottish hold and make the islands Danish again. From time to time, Denmark had made demands for the return of the islands.

A few years later the Orcadians who had resisted the force that landed got reprieve from the king for the offence of slaying the earl of Caithness and any other crimes they had committed.

In 1540 James V arrived in Orkney from Leith with twelve well-armed ships accompanied by Cardinal Beaton and other notables of Scotland. During his stay he garrisoned Kirkwall Castle, was entertained by the bishop of Orkney and then sailed on to display his authority over the Hebrides. In the following year he appointed a sheriff who had custody of the castle, an appointment which brought an end to the ancient office of lawman. In Scotland the king's castles were usually given into the keeping of sheriffs appointed by the king, whose duties were military, administrative, financial and judicial. The first sheriff of Orkney was Oliver Sinclair, a grandson of the last earl, who, although he was also tacksman of Orkney and Shetland, may never have been there. In 1542 he was taken prisoner while leading a Scottish army when it was routed by the English at Solway Moss. After hearing the news of this defeat, James V was stricken with melancholy and died soon after, leaving Mary, his one-week-old daughter, the legitimate successor to the Scottish throne.

In an attempt to secure peace for the future, a treaty was signed in 1543 by which Mary, the daughter of James V of Scotland, was to marry Edward, the son of Henry VIII of England, but it wasn't long before the Scottish parliament annulled this treaty with their old enemy and renewed their alliance with France. In anger Henry VIII sent raiding parties over the border where they devastated the countryside, destroying abbeys and burning towns. Houses in Edinburgh and Leith were burnt and the palace and abbey at Holyrood damaged. The English seized Haddington and fortified it so Scotland asked France for help. A treaty was signed in 1548 by which it was agreed that Mary should marry the dauphin and a few weeks later she sailed for France accompanied by four companions of her own age, the four Maries. Also aboard the ship was her half-brother, Robert Stewart, who was going to France to be educated. France sent a large force of well-trained soldiers for the defence of Scotland and they chased the English out. Mary of Guise, the widow of James V, now held the earldom of Orkney and she appointed a Frenchman to be governor of the castle.

This was the period when the Church of Rome was being criticised for its corruption, immorality and for the neglect of the worship in its churches. George Wishart, an early reformer, had been burnt to death at St Andrews in 1546, then John Knox, one of his followers, continued the fight. The bishoprics and monasteries had become wealthy partly through endowments and partly through a revenue paid by the parish churches. The parish churches had been placed under their care and were often allowed to fall into a ruinous condition through neglect, while some of their priests were underpaid and illiterate. Bishops and abbots were appointed by the king as an honour rather than for their devotion to the Church so most were unworthy of their appointments.

Mary of Guise was appointed queen regent and France urged her to crush the reformers who then took up arms to defend their cause, but they were no match for the French troops. Elizabeth, a daughter of Henry VIII, was now on the throne of England and she secretly supported the Scottish reformers. She had smuggled large sums of money over the border at night and some had been intercepted on behalf of the queen regent by the earl of Bothwell, warden of the Marches. Now that the reformers faced defeat, Queen Elizabeth helped them openly by sending an English fleet to the Firth of Forth to cut sea communications with France. No supplies or reinforcements could reach the queen regent, who was at Leith, so the earl of Bothwell, one of her most faithful supporters, was sent to Denmark to ask for help to defeat the blockade. Bothwell, besides being warden of the Marches, was also the hereditary admiral of Scotland, a title he had inherited from the earls of Orkney. Before Bothwell had completed his mission an English army had crossed the border into Scotland and besieged Leith but the queen regent was now in Edinburgh Castle where she had been taken after becoming ill and where she died in 1560.

Mary, the daughter of the queen regent, was now the queen of France because the dauphin whom she had married in 1558 became Francis II on the death of his father Henri II. Being the daughter of James V, Mary was Queen of Scotland and also styled herself Queen of England which would have angered Queen Elizabeth. Mary was probably persuaded to do this by France because Elizabeth wasn't recognised there as Queen of England for the Roman Catholic Church considered the marriage of Elizabeth's mother with Henry VIII to be invalid. On the early death of her husband, Francis II, Mary decided to return to Scotland and about a year after her mother, the queen regent, had died, and still only eighteen years old, she landed at Leith in a thick sea mist, accompanied by the four Maries, her ladies-in-waiting. John Knox, the reformer, an antagonist of women as well as the Church of Rome, expressed his opinion of the event when he wrote: 'The sun wasn't seen to shine two days before nor two days after.' With a Scotland in the hands of the army of the Congregation, as the reformers called themselves, and a Protestant queen on the English throne, Mary could expect little support or sympathy for the Catholic religion.

Mary's half-brother, Lord James of Moray, a leader of the Congregation, protected her from the intrigues of a country in the throes of the Reformation even though he opposed her views on religion. Another half-brother, Lord Robert, commendator of Holyrood, who had supported her mother, was now a supporter of the reformers, but he rebuilt parts of the palace at Holyrood in preparation for her arrival, it having been damaged by English raiding parties. Lord Robert was granted a lease of the crown and earldom lands in Orkney and Shetland by Mary in 1564.

Mary's second husband, Lord Darnley, was murdered in the garden of an old provost's house at Kirk o'Field in Edinburgh, where he was recovering from an illness. This house was in Cowgate, which would have then been a fashionable part of the capital, for in nearby Black Friars' Wynd a number of the nobility had houses. It was also in this part of Edinburgh that a building was bought with money left by Bishop Reid of Orkney to found a university.

In the cellar of the old provost's house where Darnley was found murdered someone had placed gunpowder, which seems to have been a popular custom about this time for a similar method was used when an attempt was made on the life of James VI, the son of Mary Queen of Scots, at the Houses of Parliament in London. A number of people were suspected of being implicated in the murder of Darnley and the earl of Bothwell was tried for it, but was acquitted through lack of evidence or because of the number of his armed followers outside the courtroom. Gilbert Balfour, master of Queen Mary's household, was accused with

Bothwell, but was pardoned, and he became governor of Kirkwall Castle. He was married to a sister of Bishop Adam Bothwell who granted him a lease of the bishopric lands in Westray. On this land is Noltland Castle, a large, grim-looking building, which could have been built for the earl of Bothwell whom Queen Mary married and created duke of Orkney, but it was never occupied by him. It had about sixty gun loops in its walls so there is no doubt that the possibility of it being attacked was considered when it was being built, no matter who was meant to occupy it. The staircase is attributed to Earl Patrick Stewart who later took possession of it.

In the morning Darnley and his manservant were found dead in the garden of the old provost's house, where they were staying, dressed in their night-clothes, so they must have made a hurried exit before the house was blown up. Nearby in the snow was Darnley's dressing gown, neatly folded, together with a pair of slippers and a chair, so it looks like a crime that Sherlock Holmes or Agatha Christie's Poirot would have had difficulty in solving.

The old provost's house was situated just inside the city wall which was then known as the Flodden Wall because it was built at the time of the battle. Near the provost's house was a gate through which any assassin could have made a quick getaway into the surrounding countryside. Queen Mary herself was suspected by some to have been implicated in the plot to kill her husband for it was known that she detested him because of the part he played in the killing of her favourite, the Italian Rizzio, in her apartments at Holyrood Palace. Queen Mary, Rizzio and Lord Robert Stewart, the future earl of Orkney, were having supper in her apartments when the murderers burst into the room, dragged Rizzio out and stabbed him to death. The part of the palace where Queen Mary had her apartments was incorporated into the new palace built by Charles II and they can be seen there today.

After the murder of Lord Darnley, James Hepburn, fourth earl of Bothwell, was created duke of Orkney by Queen Mary in May 1567 and they were married in the great hall of the Palace of Holyrood by the bishop of Orkney. One month later the army of Queen Mary and that of the reformers confronted each other at Carberry, and Mary, after persuading Bothwell to escape, surrendered. She was imprisoned in a castle which stood on an island in Loch Leven and here she was forced to renounce the throne in favour of her infant son, who was crowned at Stirling as James II of Scotland. Eleven months later she escaped from the castle in a boat and declared that the documents she had signed while imprisoned were illegal. She raised an army but was defeated at Langside near Glasgow by her half-brother, James of Moray, and she then fled over the border. In England she was the cause of plots and intrigues and when she became involved in a conspiracy to murder Queen Elizabeth of England, Elizabeth gave permission for Mary's execution which took place at Fotheringhay in 1587.

After Carberry, Bothwell fled to the north of Scotland where he collected a few ships and sailed to Orkney. He may have expected to get some help there, for Gilbert Balfour, the keeper of Kirkwall Castle, had been appointed by Mary, but he was out of luck for the guns of the castle were fired on his ships as they lay in the harbour. Bothwell went on to Shetland where he got a better welcome, but ships sent in pursuit were seen approaching, so he put to sea again and escaped across the North Sea to Norway. In Bergen, Bothwell's past caught up with him when Anna Thrond-sen, an admiral's daughter whom he had married during his visit to Denmark in 1560, took him to court for abandoning her. Anna Throndsen then lived in Bergen where her uncle, the governor, had built himself the Rosenkrantz Tower near the old hall of King Hakon V of Norway. After the court case, Bothwell was detained by Frederick II of Denmark, who may have thought he would be a valuable prisoner. Bothwell was wanted by his enemies in Scotland who had put a price on his head so maybe the king thought he could barter him for Orkney and Shetland. He had attempted to redeem them after the death of Mary of Guise but had failed. Bothwell was imprisoned in Malmo Castle which must have then belonged to Denmark and was afterwards moved to Drageholm Castle in Denmark where he died. In a church in the nearby village of Faarevejle the remains of Bothwell are now a tourist attraction as they lie on view to the public.

Philip of Spain, who had assembled a huge fleet of warships to invade England, suffered a setback when Queen Elizabeth of England sent Drake to attack Spanish warships that lay at anchor in the harbour of Cadiz. Further enraged at the execution of Queen Mary, he hurriedly completed his formidable armada and sailed for England in 1588. Drake devised a plan of attack and, when the armada entered the English Channel, he sailed from Plymouth. He found the Spanish Armada off Calais and sent eight blazing fire ships among the Spanish ships which caused them to break formation and then the guns of Drake's small ships did as much damage as they could. The armada got back into formation and proceeded on its course up the English Channel with Drake's ships in pursuit. When the armada turned into the North Sea an order was given to return to Spain by the north of Scotland. Caught in bad weather, many of the Spanish ships were wrecked; one of them, the *El Gran Grifon*, with the Duke of Medina Sidonia aboard, went aground on Fair Isle after having been blown about by the storm. In 1970 the remains of the *El Gran Grifon* were located and some cannons which were found are now in the museum at Lerwick in Shetland.

Lord Robert Stewart, an illegitimate son of James V and Euphemia Elphinstone, was married to Jean Kennedy, a daughter of the third earl of Cassillis. When he was young he got a grant of the abbacy of Holyrood which would have provided him with an income. The abbey of Holyrood had also suffered at the hands of the English and Lord Robert built himself a residence nearby with stones from the ruins. When Mary Stewart, his half-sister, arrived from France to become Queen of Scotland he was one of the few who were at Leith to welcome her and he later served her in various capacities. In 1564 she granted him a lease of the crown and earldom lands of Orkney and Shetland with the office of sheriff, which could have been a reward for services rendered. A few years later the bishop of Orkney, Adam Bothwell, was persuaded to exchange the Orkney bishopric for the abbacy of Holyrood held by Lord Robert, an arrangement which may have suited both parties for the bishop was more in the south than in his Orkney bishopric. Bishop Adam signed away his lands in Orkney at Fast Castle, a small castle perched precariously on a piece of cliff north of Berwick, a suitable place for a secretive transaction, as it seems to have been. In the exchange Lord Robert got bishopric land in Birsay and there he built his palace, probably on the site of an earlier building. Robert's palace had all the convenience as such a place in Scotland, with vegetable and flower gardens and accommodation for his attendants and servants, who were mostly Scottish. There were stables and farm buildings and a mill nearby, while at Buckquoy, a little to the north, his ships lay at anchor in a small bay. Although not built as a fortified house the palace had gun loopholes at strategic positions around its walls. Over the gateway was a stone with an inscription in Latin which stated, probably because of an error in the grammar, that he was king of Scotland, which would have made the Scottish crown apprehensive if they thought it was meant.

Lord Robert now had revenues from the bishopric as well as the earldom lands but this wasn't sufficient for his needs, so he devised ways to increase his income, as some of the previous holders of the earldom lands had done. By 1575 the islanders were complaining to the crown because he had raised their rents, altered the weights so that he got a bigger return from the land taxes which were mainly paid in farm produce, banished some of the landowners and seized their lands and altered old laws. He was also accused of treasonable negotiations with the king of Denmark and in 1576 was imprisoned in Edinburgh Castle; but two years later his nephew James VI of Scotland created him earl of Orkney, so he must have been pardoned. A son of Earl Robert, the earl of Carrick, who lived in the isle of Eday, is described in the early rentals as a 'hard craver like his father'. Earl Robert was buried in St Magnus Cathedral.

Robert's son, Patrick, succeeded as earl and he continued to oppress the people as his father had done before him. He had a flair for building and compelled his tenants to work in quarries and load stones into his ships, build dykes and other forms of manual labour without food or payment. He built a palace in Kirkwall which was known as the New Place of the Yards to distinguish it from the Bishop's Palace which was the Place of the Yards. It was said to have been the finest baronial mansion in the Scotland of that period, with its turreted windows projecting out from the walls. Within one hundred years, however, it was a ruin and it is now roofless and exposed to the weather. From the entrance, stone steps lead up to the banqueting hall where there is a huge fireplace and the remains of a large window at the south end which now overlooks a bowling green. Within a few years of it being built Earl Patrick was in prison and his palace was handed over to the bishop, so he didn't enjoy it for long. In the year 1600 Earl Patrick built Scalloway Castle in Shetland as a residence. From the entrance a stairway goes up to the first floor where the main room is and from here a spiral stairway went up to the top floor, but this will not likely be in use today. If anyone should want to go into the castle there is a key available at the nearby Shetland Wool Company's showrooms. At the corners of the castle are the remains of small turrets which must have given it a rather picturesque appearance, but to the Shetlanders who were conscripted to build it, it would have been the castle of a tyrant. Through such extravagances Earl Patrick became heavily in debt so he mortgaged a large part of his estates, chiefly to a Sir John Arnot who warned him that things were being said about him in Edinburgh.

In Scotland, fifty years after the Reformation, the new Presbyterian Church was struggling to keep itself free from royal interference, while James VI was striving to get some control over it for he disliked the independence asserted by its ministers. He was in favour of Episcopacy, a Church ruled by bishops as in England, so he bullied the General Assembly into accepting this. He appointed bishops of his own choice, this being his only hope of getting some authority in ecclesiastical affairs, and other matters evidently.

James Law, a Scottish minister, was appointed bishop of Orkney and in January 1607 an agreement was made with Earl Patrick for the bishop to be given the New Place of the Yards as a residence. When Bishop Law arrived he became aware of the oppression the islanders were living under and he sent a complaint to the king. The earl was summoned to Edinburgh where he was imprisoned in the castle and the earldom was taken over by the crown. On payment of a surety by friends, Earl Patrick was released, but when he sent his son Robert north on the pretence of collecting arrears of rent, he was rearrested and imprisoned in Dumbarton Castle.

In 1610, by an act of parliament, all foreign laws in Orkney and Shetland had been abolished while in 1612 another act annexed the earldom of Orkney and lordship of Shetland to the Scottish crown again. Bishop Law, who had been appointed to be His Majesty's commissioner, sheriff and justice, held a court in St Magnus Cathedral on 30 July 1612 when four bailies and eight councillors were sworn in and sundry acts passed. On 10 August he held a sheriff's court in Sumburgh House, Shetland, and on 21 August he sat in judgement at a court in the hall of Scalloway Castle.

Robert Stewart had been ejected from Orkney and he visited his father at Dumbarton Castle. Earl Patrick, raging with fury at his son for having given in to the bishop, now urged him to return. Robert, who was loyal to and dominated by his father, went to Orkney again in May 1614 and with a few friends took possession of Birsay Palace. He then recruited some local Orcadians and with his band of followers he marched to Kirkwall and without much resistance seized the castle, the cathedral and the palace. The earl of Caithness, who was in Edinburgh at the time, got the job of quelling the rebellion and with a company of soldiers and some cannon from Edinburgh Castle he sailed from Leith during the month of August.

The earl began to disembark his troops at Carness near Kirkwall and Robert Stewart marched to oppose the landing, but after advancing with his ensign flying and drums beating, he halted, fired a volley, then he and some of the rebels took refuge in the castle, the cathedral tower and the palace, while the remainder dispersed and returned to their homes. The earl of Caithness began the operation by dragging his big guns into position and opening fire on the rebels, and Robert with the rebels who were in the cathedral and palace considered it wise to seek shelter in the castle. The thick walls of the castle withstood the cannon fire for three weeks and the earl of Caithness wrote: 'The house had never been built without the consent of the devil for it is one of the strongest holds in Britain.' He also wrote that his cannon balls broke in two like golf balls. The rebels were eventually induced to surrender by the offer of a pardon which they didn't receive, for Robert and most of his followers were hanged while Patrick Halcro, who had attempted to negotiate with the earl of Caithness, was pardoned. The government ordered the castle to be destroyed while the cathedral escaped a similar fate on the intervention of the bishop of Orkney. The king tried to persuade Earl Patrick to renounce his rights to the earldom, but as he refused he was beheaded at the Mercat Cross in Edinburgh by the Maiden, an early type of guillotine.

Two More Centuries of Hardship

Orkney had now been mortgaged to Scotland for over a century and, although the Scottish government had promised to preserve the Norse laws and customs, in 1541 the appointment of a lawman, an official who had existed since Norse times and who had presided at courts and affixed the common seal of the islands to important documents, was ended. In his place a Scottish sheriff was appointed. Robert Stewart, when he was earl, is said to have been responsible for ending one old custom, that of grinding corn with hand-operated quern mills, by decreeing that corn was to be taken to a mill where the miller would be paid a multure, a portion of the corn for his services. Earl Robert is believed to have owned a number of mills, so if the above is correct, it could have been another scheme to increase his income.

The hand-operated quern mill, which had been in use for centuries, was a device for grinding grain by rotating the upper stone with one hand by means of a wooden handle, while the other hand fed grain into a round opening at its centre. On the underside of the upper stone, on either side of the opening, there were two grooves into which was fitted a piece of hard wood to support the upper stone on a spindle. The spindle must have fitted into the hard wood and would have been fixed into the lower stone. When a coarse end product was required, a washer was fitted on the spindle, between the stones, to raise the upper one. Some querns had a more sophisticate method for raising the upper stone, which was by a wood bar underneath. The underside of the top stone was slightly concave while the top of the under stone was convex so that one fitted over the other. Lines radiating from the centre were cut into the surface of both stones which would have made it easier for the grain to work its way towards the edges of the stones where the grain would have been collected on a cloth spread out underneath the quern.

Fifty years ago you could see small round stones, some noticeably with holes in them, adorning the outside walls of some Orkney houses. These were, I presume, quern stones from a past era. When on a visit to Shetland recently I noticed two mill stones along the wall of a farmhouse there. These were larger than quern stones but appeared to be smaller than ordinary mill stones. These would have been from Shetland mills which had been situated on small streams where there wouldn't have been enough water to drive large mill stones.

After the Stewart period the earldom and bishopric lands were interchanged for the sake of convenience. The bishopric land had been intermixed with the earldom land in the various islands, in the same parishes and even in the same farms, so to remedy this Bishop Law was given seven and a half parishes conveniently situated on Mainland and on nearby islands. These were to be exclusively bishopric and were to have the same value of rents, skats and teinds[1] as the former church lands had. When Bishop Law arrived in Orkney he found the Bishop's Palace in ruins and Earl Patrick allowed him to reside in the New Place of the Yards, the palace built by Earl Patrick. This also became the residence of the next bishop, Bishop Graeme, when Bishop Law left Orkney after being appointed archbishop of Glasgow.

Besides being a churchman, Bishop Graeme had an interest in finance. He acquired for himself Skaill in Sandwick while his youngest son got Breckness in Stromness parish. At the extreme west of Stromness parish, overlooking the Atlantic, is the Black Craig. It was here, during the month of March 1834, that a schooner drifted on to the rocks during a storm and the only survivor was washed into a cave where he spent three days before climbing to the top of the cliff.

Skaill Bay and Skaill are in a gap of cliffs which stretch north from the Black Craig to Marwick Head. During Norse times Skaill was a bu, the principal farm in the area, where a chieftain would have lived, with a sandy beach nearby where he could draw up his longship. Not far from Skaill is the Stone Age village of Skara Brae which, as the house of Skaill, is open to the public. Another son of Bishop Graeme had property in Holm which he

---

[1] This was a tax levied for the upkeep of the church.

renamed Graemeshall. The direct line of the Graemes of Graemeshall ended with an Admiral Alexander Sutherland Graeme,
who like Nelson had lost his right arm. Bishop Graeme was
deposed after the Presbyterians revolted against Episcopacy in
1638.

In 1622 James Stewart of Kilsyth, who was also known as Lord
Ochiltree, was deprived of his lease because of oppression. The
islanders must have become accustomed to such treatment from
their Scottish leaseholders who all seem to have been determined
to make as much profit as possible from their holding. Most of the
inhabitants of Scotland seem to have suffered the same sort of
servitude although the leaseholders in Orkney could have taken
more liberties being further away from the seat of government.
During the next twenty years there was a number of lessees who
made what profit they could, with little interest in improving the
lot of their tenants.

Charles I was now king and when on a visit to Scotland he
noted the simplicity of the church services there and, thinking
there was need for improvement, he tried to impose a revised
prayer book on the Scots. The Presbyterians resented this and
nobles, lairds, burgesses and ministers alike signed a National
Covenant pledging to uphold the Presbyterian form of worship,
while a General Assembly deposed the bishops and abolished
Episcopacy. The General Assembly had authority over Church
affairs. The bishop of Orkney, George Graeme was deposed, and
the bishopric rents were granted by Parliament to the city of
Edinburgh.

The Covenanters in Scotland now prepared another covenant
which aimed at getting a uniformity of religion in all of Great
Britain. They joined forces with the Puritans of England and in
1644 helped them to defeat the royalist army under Prince Rupert
at Marston Moor near Richmond, Yorkshire. James Graham, the
earl of Montrose, had signed the National Covenant, but now that
the Covenanters had sided against the king he changed sides and
was given command of the royalist forces in Scotland and created
marquis by King Charles. Although a relative of Bishop George
Graeme of Orkney, the marquis is usually referred to as James
Graham which is a different version of the same surname. With

only a small following he won several victories before being surprised and defeated by the Covenanter General Leslie at Philiphaugh in 1645. Montrose escaped with a small party of horse troops after having hacked a way through the enemy, then after a few years in exile, during which time Charles I was executed, he arrived back in Scotland. The time Montrose chose had seemed favourable because Cromwell was in Ireland, but the help from Scotland which he had expected didn't materialise and the venture turned out to be ill-advised.

On a document dated 1633 Charles I is said to be styled earl of Orkney, and in the same year, while present at the Scottish parliament, he gave three hundred pounds for repairs to St Magnus Cathedral. He had leased the crown possessions in Orkney to a William, earl of Morton, who may have invited Montrose to use Orkney as a base to assemble his army before invading Scotland. During the autumn of 1649 two ships sailed from Gothenburg in Sweden carrying some continental troops, but these were lost when the ships were wrecked on the rocks of the islands during a storm. A few weeks later two more ships carrying more troops, as well as the earl of Kinnoul and his brother, arrived safely. Kinnoul made his headquarters at Birsay Palace while his troops were quartered throughout Mainland.

In the spring of the following year the beacon fires gave warning of approaching ships. The warning beacons, which were on the highest hills, were kept supplied with peat and heather even at this date, for Kirkwall was often attacked and plundered by warships. On this occasion, however, they were friendly for they carried the earl of Montrose, accompanied by some of his officers and about two hundred continental volunteers. At first Montrose stayed in the Earl's Palace at Kirkwall then he moved to Noltland Castle in Westray, and in April he mustered his army, which now numbered over two thousand men, for he had enlisted some recruits since he arrived in the islands. They all embarked at Holm, and on landing in Caithness Montrose displayed his banners. The news of the landing soon spread. When it reached Dunbeath, Sir John Sinclair of that ilk took horse for Edinburgh to give warning of the invasion while Montrose proceeded to Thurso and summoned the lairds of the county to swear an oath of allegiance to him and the royal cause. On his way south Montrose besieged Dunbeath Castle which, like other castles on that coast, was situated on a high cliff. After holding out for a few days the castle surrendered and Montrose placed a garrison in it, then continued on to the Ord. He met no resistance until he reached Carbisdale on the border of Sutherlandshire and Ross-shire, where his progress was checked by a detachment of cavalry troops riding in advance of General Leslie who had been sent north by the government. The continental troops made a stand but his untrained infantry recruits fled before the charging cavalry, and Montrose with two companions made their escape into the nearby scrub. After crossing the River Orkell they took to the hills where, after wandering for several days without food or water, Montrose and one of his companions were apprehended and handed over to the Covenanters who executed them in Edinburgh. Most of the Orcadians were either slain or drowned in the fast-flowing River Orkell.

In punishment for assisting Montrose, General Leslie sent a company of horse troops to Orkney where they quartered themselves on the inhabitants and destroyed the crops growing in the fields. Cromwell sent soldiers of the Commonwealth there, and they built a fort on the eastern outskirts of Kirkwall. Horses and money were demanded from the people, while English warships plundered the islands. Patrick Balfour, the owner of Noltland Castle in Westray where Montrose had stayed for a time, was fined two thousand pounds. On the credit side, however, Cromwell's soldiers are said to have taught the Orcadians improved methods of agriculture and how to make locks and keys, while some of them married and settled in the islands.

The Commonwealth period ended after the death of Cromwell when Charles II was proclaimed king and Episcopacy was revived. The city of Edinburgh had been granted the Orkney bishopric and now had to surrender it up to the crown, while the duty paid on all wines and liquor sold within the burgh of Edinburgh and nearby Leith was given to the city as compensation. The islands were again annexed to the crown and over the next thirty years were rented on short leases to a number of lessees who as before made what profit they could. Fort Charlotte in Lerwick was built during the reign of Charles II on a high spot overlooking the harbour.

The duke of Monmouth, an illegitimate son of Charles II, conspired with the duke of Argyll and other exiled Scots in Rotterdam to get himself crowned king. The duke of Argyll was to land in Scotland and Monmouth in England. Argyll sailed to Orkney where two men were put ashore as emissaries but these were taken prisoner and because of this the government became aware of the uprising. Argyll was captured in Scotland and executed while Monmouth was defeated at Sedgemoor and then executed. The duke of Monmouth had been in command of the royalist army which had defeated the Scottish Covenanters at Bothwell Bridge. Some of the Covenanters taken prisoner at this battle were drowned when the ship taking them to the American colonies sank at Deerness in Orkney where a monument commemorates the event near the spot where it happened.

When Charles II died in 1685 he was succeeded by his brother James who fled to France when the Protestant, William of Orange, the son of a sister of Charles II, landed in England three years later. William became king and he re-established the Presbyterian Church which has remained the established Church of Scotland ever since. In 1696 the title earl of Orkney was bestowed on Lieutenant General Lord George Hamilton, a famous soldier in Marlborough's time. In 1706 Queen Anne granted the earldom estates to James, earl of Morton, as a pledge for thirty thousand pounds sterling, a debt the crown owed the earls of Morton. This grant was later made irredeemable, but after years of disputes with the landholders the earl of Morton sold the rights to a Sir Lawrence Dundas, the baronet of Kerse. In the beginning of this century the Dundas family, like other landowners in the islands, sold their land mainly to the tenants. The bishopric estates which were returned to the crown when William of Orange became king seem to have been leased on short leases to various tacksmen. In 1775 they were granted to Lord Dundas, a son of Sir Lawrence.

At this period methods of agriculture in Scotland were very unproductive and farm implements very laborious to use and gave little result. As it had been for generations, arable land was divided into portions which were separated by baulks, strips of grass left unploughed. This was known as runrig, and each portion would have a different owner. An ancient type of plough, made almost entirely of wood, which made a furrow only a few inches deep, was still being used.[2] After the union with England in 1707, more productive methods of agriculture moved over the border into Scotland. Turnips were introduced and used as a winter feed for the cattle, while potatoes, clovers and ryegrass for fodder were introduced a little later. An iron plough which turned over the soil with less effort and which required only two horses to pull it and one man to manage replaced the wooden plough which needed three men and at least four horses or oxen. Some of the tacksmen or middlemen had houses built of dressed stone, with slate roofs, glass windows, wooden floors and chimneys. Coal was beginning to displace peat, but any change took some time to penetrate the Highlands for the Highlander was reluctant to alter the ways of his ancestors. He still built his home with undressed stone, and used timber and turf or heather for the roof, a type of house known in the Hebrides as a black-house. He grew oats and bere, an inferior type of barley, but the crops were poor and in winter the animals were underfed. In the summer the cattle and sheep were pastured at the shielings, the hill grazings. The majority of the landholders were tenants who had only a few acres of land which they dug with spades. The potato, however, had reached the Highlands and it began to take the place of oats and bere as it gave a high yield and it became the main subsistence of the Highlander.

Towards the end of the eighteenth century, black-faced sheep were introduced into Scotland for large-scale sheep rearing. The project started off with good intent, and it filled up the empty hills of the Highlands, but when the sheep farmers wanted more land to graze the sheep on, they offered the landowners higher rents. This didn't help the Highlander tenant for he was cleared out of the glens, some being given small crofts near the coast where they had to live on potatoes and any fish they could catch, while others were encouraged to emigrate.

---

[2] A plough of this type can be seen in the Tankerness Museum in Kirkwall.

Although Caithness may not have been affected by the clearances as badly as Sutherland and other parts of the Highlands and islands, the tenants there were said to have been subjected to what could almost be called slavery, for besides paying a rent and a small teind to the vicarage they had to perform numerous services for the laird such as ploughing, manuring, sowing, weeding, thatching and carrying peat. Caithness has large stretches of fertile land and, as it had a relatively small population, more agricultural produce was grown there than it required for its own consumption, so it exported the surplus. Even before the union with England, large quantities of malt and meal was shipped to the Baltic from the port of Thurso. Before carts were introduced into the county, two wicker baskets, fastened on either side of a wooden saddle which rested on a straw cushion on the back of a small horse, served the purpose. Grain was transported in straw bags called cazies, which were also fastened on either side of a horse's saddle. During the eighteenth century whisky was distilled and it took the place of ale as the popular drink. Snuff made from tobacco imported from America found its way there at an early date. In 1655 a member of a congregation in Canisbay was fined for taking snuff during a service, but the habit prevailed and many elderly men and women, and younger persons also, carried snuff boxes.

At the beginning of the nineteenth century agriculture in the islands hadn't changed much. They were still using a one-stilted wooden plough which could be cheaply purchased and the arable land was still divided up according to the old runrig system. Farms were generally small and most tenants didn't have a lease and paid their rent in kind: corn for the arable land and butter for pasture. Farms that lay next to the sea had the foreshore allotted to them, which is a right they have had since Norse times, and from this piece of shore, seaweed was cut to use as fertiliser on the land. Common land which belonged to the community and which was separated from the farming land by a turf dyke was used to graze the livestock on during the summer. In September the corn was cut with what the Reverend George Barry described as a blunt hook, which like the one-stilted plough was of little use. The blunt hook or reaping hook would have probably been a sickle, a small implement with a semicircular blade. The cut corn was made into loosely bound sheaves which were spread out at the base and stood up a few together to dry. The dry corn was taken to the farmyard where it was built into small stacks on wooden bases and then taken into the barn for threshing. Some gentlemen farmers had enclosed their farms with stone dykes, dug ditches for drainage purposes and were using a two-stilted plough and iron teethed harrows and in so doing produced better crops. During the past fifty years potatoes had been grown on almost every farm, for their own use and for sale. Some turnips were grown as winter feed for the small black cattle which seem to have been popular at this period, while for fodder, ryegrass and clover had been tried. After an inquiry by the Board of Agriculture in 1794, it was found to have been the custom to alternate yearly the main crops, which were bere-barley and oats, and this had been done for centuries past. This was crop rotation, a policy that the board was recommending farmers to adopt.

The farmhouse of this period had been built to withstand the high winds of the islands so had low, thick stone walls with a roof of flagstones, or a thatched roof of twisted heather or grass. Part of the house usually accommodated the animals which sometimes used the same door as the human occupants. The floor would have been of earth or flagstones and in the centre a peat fire would have burnt against a free-standing stone, which divided the room into two parts: a but and a ben. The ben-end was the sleeping quarters, and would have contained a box bed, a bed that was enclosed on all sides except at the front where there was a folding wooden door. At the roof ridge there was a lum, a hole about one foot square, which allowed the smoke from the peat fire to escape after it had hung about a while coating the rafters and roof with soot. To prevent the smoke from being blown back down the lum, a wood board, which could be moved to windward, was fitted outside the hole. Somewhere in the roof there was a skylight to let some light in during the day, while at night a cruisie lamp would be lit and the light from this together with the glow from the peat fire would probable give sufficient illumination to allow people to move about. The cruisie lamp was made entirely of metal and had two long spouted saucers, one placed over the other. The top saucer could be tilted so that the fish oil which it usually held could run along the spout where there was a wick, usually the pith of a rush. The wick projected over the end of the spout of the top saucer and any drops of oil were caught by the lower saucer. To sit on, there would be a pair of straw-backed chairs, probably with straw hoods to give some protection from any draughts.

In the year 1668 a small square-rigged ketch, the *Nonsuch*, was sent to the Hudson Bay in North America to investigate the possibility of trading with the natives and for exploration purposes. Two years later in 1670 the Hudson Bay Company was founded with permission from Charles II to trade in territory bordering the Hudson Bay. Prince Rupert, the king's cousin, who had fought against the Covenanters, became its first governor and he had large tracts of land in that part of North America named after him. The company established its first trading post in Ontario and the Indians brought furs, mainly beaver, which were the most valuable, down the rivers to trade them for axes, blankets, fishing tackle and flour. As trade increased the company pushed further inland to set up trading posts nearer the trapping grounds and like the Indians the company's men travelled by birch canoe, having to negotiate dangerous rapids and cross large lakes on the way. Towards the end of the seventeenth century England was at war with France and ships of the Hudson Bay Company took a route around the north of Scotland to avoid enemy pirates and warships. They made Stromness their last port of call before crossing the Atlantic and it continued to be so for almost two centuries. They called in the early summer, stocked up with water and provisions while waiting for a favourable wind, and took aboard the Orcadians they had recruited to work for them. In the autumn they returned with the men who had finished their term of service, which was five years, and would have probably also carried that year's consignment of furs. Besides supplying provisions, Stromness also sent articles of clothing and other necessities, a trade which continued up to the end of the nineteenth century. Some of the Hudson Bay men from Orkney settled in North America, one being a James Dreaver of Westray who had worked for the company in 1845. He married a daughter of a Cree Indian chief and his grandson became chief of the Cree Indians. According to a Canadian TV film shown in this country, at the south part of the Hudson Bay where the company first operated, there are many descendants of Hudson Bay men among the Cree Indians who live there. The tartan is popular with them and some are expert at playing Scottish tunes on the fiddle.

In the year 1725 a square-sterned ship with mounted guns dropped anchor in Cairston Roads. It was not engaged in legitimate business for its captain was the pirate John Gow, who had spent his boyhood in Stromness before going to sea in his father's trading sloops. His father was a Caithness merchant who had settled in Stromness and built a house there. John Gow's stay was short-lived for his identity became known and he deemed it wise to make a hurried departure. He sailed northwards and while taking his ship between Eday and the Calf of Eday, where there is a strong tide-race, it ran aground. Gow and his crew were captured through some strategy devised by James Fea of Stronsay who was staying at Carrick House in Eday at the time and they were disarmed. After being tried in London Gow and seven of his crew were hanged. When Walter Scott visited Stromness in 1814 he saw a character called Bessie Millie who was living in a hovel on the sheltered side of Brinkie's Brae and who sold 'favourable winds' to mariners at sixpence a time. She was then over ninety years old and remembered Gow the pirate when she was a girl. The exploits of Gow when in Orkney inspired Scott to write his novel *The Pirate*, in which Captain Cleveland is the pirate while Norna of Fitful Read in Shetland is said to have been based on Bessie Millie. In the notes to *The Pirate*, Walter Scott states that it was a venturous master mariner who left the harbour of Stromness without visiting Bessie Millie, who claimed that the wind bought for the moderate fee of sixpence was sure to arrive, but the mariners sometimes had to wait a while for it.

It was because of war that Stromness grew in importance, for merchant ships going round the north of Scotland took shelter in its harbour and found carpenters and shipwrights there who could carry out repairs. Stromness became a thriving sea port and inns sprung up for the benefit of the mariners, supplied no doubt by a brewery that was there about at that time. Ships brought cargoes for the Stromness merchants, while other vessels sheltered there and took on board water and stores. In 1780 it had the privilege of accommodating the two ships of Captain Cook's expedition. They were the *Discovery* and *Resolution* and they had been driven northwards from the English Channel by contrary winds. While in the Hawaiian Islands, Captain Cook had been killed by the natives. Whalers heading for the Arctic sea called and while there engaged Orcadians to complete their crews. Hunting the whale was then a hazardous business for it necessitated harpooning it at close quarters from small boats. During the Napoleonic Wars, Stromness had been prosperous, but when the war ended and shipping returned to its normal routes again some merchants went out of business because fewer ships made it a port of call. In fifty years its population had doubled but now it began to decrease and maybe the passing of the sailing ship helped in this decline in importance.

In 1742 merchants of the then village of Stromness paid a tax to the royal burgh of Kirkwall for the privilege of participating in foreign trade and Stromness was not alone in this for the tax was exacted by royal burghs throughout Scotland. A number of independently minded Stromness merchants refused to pay the tax and this grew into a big legal battle. At first the court decided in favour of Kirkwall, then Stromness appealed to a higher court which reversed the decision. The convention of Royal Burghs backed Kirkwall and as the outcome would have far-reaching consequences for them, they took the case to the House of Lords. The Lords decided in favour of the Stromness merchants, a decision which freed villages throughout Scotland from paying tax to neighbouring royal burghs. The dispute left Alexander Graham, a wealthy Stromness merchant, bankrupt, as he evidently alone had to foot the bill for Stromness's legal costs.

The eighteenth century started off during a spell of very cold weather which lasted for seven years and this resulted in famine as the crops didn't ripen again. A third of the population of Midlothian are said to have died during the famine, so the percentage of fatalities in the north of Scotland would probably have been higher; Orkney may not have suffered so severely as it has milder winters. Survivors of this famine period had to assemble under their chiefs when the Highland clans joined the earl of Mar at the time of the 1715 Jacobite rebellion, a rising that was short-lived.

When Queen Anne, the last of the Stuart monarchs, died in 1714, parliament settled for George of Hanover as her successor. The earl of Mar, out of favour with the new king, suggested at a meeting at Braemar that the son of James VII would be a better choice for a king and, finding support, he soon had an army of twelve thousand clansmen. With these he met a government force under the duke of Argyll at Sheriffmuir a few miles north of Dunblane, a battle that proved indecisive. A charge by the Highlanders routed the left wing of Argyll's army, but on the other side of the field the English cavalry scattered the Highlanders. Argyll fell back to Dunblane and the earl of Mar to Perth, where he met the son of James VII, better known as the Old Pretender, who had been delayed by bad weather, on his way from France. By now the rising was about over, for part of the Scottish army had been defeated in England while most of Mar's Highlanders had departed for their homes laden with booty. With Argyll now in pursuit, the earl of Mar withdrew to Dundee, across the River Tay which was frozen over by another spell of very cold weather; then after dismissing his army he and the Old Pretender sailed to France from Montrose aboard the *Marie Therese*.

About fifty of the leading rebels had their estates forfeited, there were many executions and an attempt was made to disarm the clansmen. When another rising took place in the west of Scotland during 1719, with foreign aid, the government took stronger action. Loyal clansmen were recruited to patrol the Highlands and they became known as the Black Watch, a name which remained with them when they were later formed into a regiment. Fort Augustus was built at the southern extremity of Loch Ness and General Wade, the commander-in-chief in Scotland, built roads and bridges throughout the Highlands so that his troops could move about more quickly. Some present-day roads follow stretches of these old roads such as the one that crosses the River Tay at Aberfeldy by a bridge that Wade built there in 1733 and the road from Fort William to Fort Augustus. There was peace in the Highlands for twenty-five years and then clansmen had to suffer and die again in another Jacobite rising after they joined Prince Charles Edward when he landed in Scotland in 1745.

The story of how the prince unfurled his standard at Glenfinnan and claimed the throne of Great Britain for his father, the Old Pretender, is well known. Reluctant at first, the clansmen were soon joining the prince's small army as he marched to Perth. Edinburgh was captured and the prince held a levee in the long gallery at Holyrood, while the castle at the other end of the city was held by the government. Shortly afterwards the Highlanders defeated Cope at Prestonpans after a strategic approach during the night and six weeks later the prince started on a forlorn march south. At Derby his generals persuaded him to return to Scotland for the English armies outnumbered his small force, so the prince made a reluctant retreat to Carlisle with the English at his rear. Back in Scotland the Jacobite army defeated an equal-sized government force at Falkirk before heading for the Highlands where they captured Ruthven Barracks in Badenoch. By the spring of 1746 the duke of Cumberland was in the north-east of Scotland with a larger and better equipped government army. He took control of the ports on the north-east coast, while English ships patrolled Scottish seas, some finding an anchorage in Cairston Roads, Stromness. A ship carrying gold sovereigns for the prince, all the help he could get from France, found English warships in the Moray Firth where it was to make a landing, so it headed north and entered the Pentland Firth. Here its captain found out that one of the English warships was in pursuit so he took his ship into the Kyle of Tongue in Sutherland, hoping the water there would be too shallow for the larger ship, but it got near enough to get its guns within range and in a few hours the French ship was a total wreck. Cumberland's redcoats were fresh and well fed but the prince's army was exhausted through long marches and hunger which the lost sovereigns would have helped to alleviate. At Culloden Moor near Inverness the prince decided to make a stand, being tired of avoiding Cumberland's army, and the redcoats cut the Highlanders to pieces. The terrain at Culloden hadn't suited the Highlanders for they preferred to attack from a vantage point from where they could charge down, shouting their battle cries to unnerve the enemy, but the prince had insisted that they should make a stand there. Although the government offered a large reward for the capture of Prince Charles, no one jumped at the bait and he reached Benbecula in the Hebrides. From there he made his famous escape from searching redcoats with Flora MacDonald, dressed as her servant, and eventually boarded a French ship at Loch nan Uamh.

Not many in the north of Scotland had supported the rebellion, but many of the ladies are said to have worn a miniature of the prince around their necks. Some lairds in Orkney had their homes burnt down by government marines, so they must have been, or were suspected of being, Jacobites. James Stewart, the laird of Burray, on returning to Orkney after taking part in the rising, was captured by a son of a Captain Moodie of Melsetter. Captain Moodie had been killed in Kirkwall during a quarrel with James of Burray some years previously, so there would have been a motive of revenge connected with the capture. James of Burray was taken to London where he died in prison while awaiting trial, and he was the last of the Stewarts of Burray.

After Culloden the duke of Cumberland savagely suppressed the Jacobites, using the bayonet, and he burnt down their homes as was done in Orkney. There were more executions and hangings and more estates forfeited, while the Highlanders were again disarmed, but there may have been many good weapons hidden away and a lot of rusty ones handed in, as is said to have been done at other times. The kilt was banned and in 1741 parliament passed an act which abolished hereditary jurisdiction. This was a feudal custom by which a lord or clan chief ruled his land with the authority to hold his own courts and administer justice without interference from the crown. Abolishing this would have been done to weaken the authority of the clan chief over his clan, but the influence of the chiefs was more personal. The earl of Morton who was granted Orkney and Shetland by Queen Anne was granted also hereditary jurisdiction. Maybe the Stewart earls were given the same privilege, which would have allowed them to impose unfair sentences in the courts without fear of interference from the crown but being so remote that would have been difficult in any case. Cromwell abolished hereditary jurisdiction, but it was re-established at the Restoration. The act of 1747, however, ended it for good.

The Islands Begin to Prosper

When the nineteenth century started, Britain was at war with France and many Orcadians were press-ganged into the navy at this time. On either side of the entrance to Longhope small forts were built to protect the inlet against enemy warships for merchant ships assembled there while they waited to sail in convoys under armed escorts. These forts are called Martello towers and many were built along the south coast of England during the Napoleonic Wars. They are round and have walls six feet thick so have something in common with the brochs; the idea for them came from forts seen in Corsica, where it is suggested the brochs originated. When seaweed is burnt a substance called kelp can be produced, and from it chemicals which manufacturers use to make glass and soap can be obtained. When chemicals became scarce during the war, Orkney made a lot of money by producing kelp and selling it to the manufacturers. When the war ended, however, the chemicals which had become scarce during the war could be obtained again, so the production of kelp in Orkney fell off, but seaweed was still collected for the iodine it contained and for use as a fertiliser. Some farmers had been neglecting the land for the more profitable kelp so they now turned back to farming and started to use more modern methods of agriculture.

The old runrig custom of dividing up the land was in the process of being done away with and fields of a reasonable size were taking the place of the small strips. Tenants who were willing to use methods of farming that had been successful in the south were put in the new-style holdings. To create these new farms some crofters were moved from their crofts and were given wasteland which required a lot of toil before anything could be cultivated, so the changes were not very popular. Some landlords sold farms to former tenants, while others got leases. This encouraged the tenants improve the farms and better breeds of horses, cattle and sheep were introduced into the islands. Crops were rotated and the harvesting was speeded up by using reaping machines instead of the sickle or reaping hook mentioned in the previous chapter, while threshing mills took the place of flails. In the south, crushed bones and chemicals were used as fertilisers and oilcake as cattle feed so these could also have helped farming in the north of Scotland.

In 1833 a steamship service was started between Leith and Kirkwall via Aberdeen which helped farming in Orkney for it gave an easier access to the south. In 1840 some areas were still using the runrig land division, but by the middle of the century, when the improvements were more widespread and beginning to take effect, farming started to flourish and there was a change from a poverty-stricken condition to prosperity. In 1861 the population of the islands reached a peak of over thirty thousand and from that time there was a gradual decrease to its present figure of about twenty thousand.

In 1789, a lighthouse was built at Dennis Point, North Ronaldsay, a structure which is still standing though not in use now. Many ships were wrecked on the outlying skerries of North Ronaldsay which is a low-lying island and the most northern of the Orkney Islands. In 1794 a lighthouse was erected on Muckle Skerry in the Pentland Firth. When this one was built, it was calculated that over three thousand ships passed through the Pentland Firth annually even though it is a dangerous stretch of water with strong currents swirling beneath its surface. A lighthouse flashing on a headland or a beacon winking on a skerry warns ships to keep clear, but a lighthouse can act as a guide. In 1851 Hoy High and Hoy Low lighthouses on Graemsay were completed, and when a ship enters Hoy Sound from the Atlantic and has the two lights in line, it is on a correct course so that it avoids such obstacles as the Kirk Rocks near the shore of Innertown, Stromness, where a number of ships have been wrecked. In 1867 the Lifeboat Institute sent Stromness a thirty-three feet longboat called the *Saltaire*. A slipway and shed to house it were built at the Point of Ness, but this location was found to be unsuitable as it was too exposed, so the lifeboat rode at anchor in the harbour of Stromness until a more sheltered site was found for it.

Early in the nineteenth century, Orkney traded with the ports of Aberdeen, Leith and Liverpool, mainly by sailing smacks, and sailing ships continued in use after the steamer service started. The first steamship to reach Orkney was a wooden paddle steamer owned by the Aberdeen, Leith and Clyde Shipping Company which arrived at Kirkwall in 1833. This company started its existence in 1790 as the Leith and Clyde Shipping Company, which was the same year that the Forth-Clyde canal opened, so the company probably operated on the canal. In 1810 they amalgamated with the Aberdeen, Dundee and Leith Shipping Company when they would have extended their sailings to Aberdeen. After they had acquired two paddle steamers and extended their sailings further north they became the North of Scotland, Orkney and Shetland Steam Navigation Company.

This would have been after one of their paddle steamers arrived at Lerwick in Shetland in 1836. At first they only ran a summer service but in 1861 a new ship, an iron-built, screw-driven steamer called the *Queen II* did the trip to Shetland in winter which would have heralded a winter steamer service as well as the summer one. Orkney got a boost to its economy when the steamer service started, because of reduced freight charges, while Shetland's economy started to improve when the Queen's Hotel was opened near Lerwick harbour in 1864 which was only a few years after the steamship *Queen II* had arrived at Lerwick, so it seems possible that the hotel was named after the ship. At the turn of the century the North of Scotland Shipping Company opened the St Magnus Hotel at Hillswick in Shetland after which time they promoted cruises with a stay at Hillswick.

During the First World War the company lost two ships through enemy action. The *St Margaret* was torpedoed thirty miles east of the Faeroes, while the *St Magnus* was sunk off Peterhead. Between the wars three of the older ships were replaced by larger vessels, and an extra one, the *St Clement*, a cargo boat, was added to the fleet. In 1939, to make up for the loss of tonnage due to ships being requisitioned by the government, the company acquired the *Highlander*, a ship which was built in 1916 for the Aberdeen, Newcastle and Hull Shipping Company. In August 1940 the *Highlander* was sailing in a small convoy bound for Leith when the convoy was attacked by ten Heinkel bombers. The *Highlander*'s gunners shot down two of the German bombers and one fell on to the ship's poop, so she steamed into Leith with this memento of the attack. After this achievement, the *Highlander* was renamed *St Catherine II* for it was considered she was now a marked ship, and after surviving two more attacks she was sunk off Aberdeen with the loss of a Captain Norquay, thirteen members of the crew and one passenger. Many years ago I sailed in her from the Newcastle quay to Aberdeen and then by the *St Rognvald II* to Orkney. Sea travel then, as now, was a cheap way to travel, especially steerage or second class, which in the *St Rognvald*, if my memory doesn't err, was in the forecastle where there were bunks in tiers like some wartime army billets, cattle in a nearby hold and sheep penned on the deck outside. The *St Rognvald II*, however, was a reliable ship which saw fifty years of service with the company. The *St Rognvald III* was a motor cargo vessel, carrying livestock and a few passengers and it differed from the other ships as its bridge and accommodation were aft.

About this time a three-thousand-ton drive-on drive-off ferry was built to replace the *St Clair III* on the Aberdeen to Lerwick run and the Leith to Aberdeen part of their sailing schedule was axed and some ships were disposed of; one, the *St Ninian*, was a ship that must have been well known. The North of Scotland, Orkney and Shetland Shipping Company Limited, as the company was now named, became a subsidiary of the Peninsular and Orient Steam Navigation Company who operate in the north of Scotland as P & O Scottish Ferries. Ships of P & O Scottish Ferries berth at Jamieson's Quay at Aberdeen which is conveniently near the railway station for anyone who travels that way. In Shetland P & O Ferries have built a terminal at the north end of Lerwick and adjacent to it is the new luxury Shetland Hotel which will be conveniently near for passengers coming off the ferries. Outside the entrance of the hotel is a cannon which belonged to a Dutch ship that was probably sunk by guns of Fort Charlotte which overlooks the harbour. To the north of Lerwick is Gremista, where Arthur Anderson, one of the co-founders of the Peninsular Steamship Company, was born and the house is now a museum to his memory. In 1837 the shipping company he helped to found became the Peninsular and Orient Steam Navigation Company, so P & O Ferries can claim that one of their founders was born near their most northern berthing place. At the south end of Lerwick there are some old merchants' houses at the water's edge, each with a small landing place which was used for unloading merchandise and which was called a lodberry. A little further down the road is a row of houses occupied by seamen's widows, given by Arthur Anderson, and also at the south end is the academy he founded.

Early in the nineteenth century a commission was set up to organise the building of roads and bridges in the north of Scotland. In 1769, Pennant, a visitor to Caithness stated that there wasn't a cart track or a mile of road that could be properly so called in that county and that the whole district was an immense morass with a few spots where oats and barley were being cultivated. This was now being changed, for roads were being built under the supervision of the Scottish engineer Thomas Telford and agriculture was improving. By 1819 a stagecoach carrying mail and passengers was running along a road from the Ord in the south of Caithness to Wick and Thurso in the north, but there was no proper road to Huna in Duncansby from where a ferry boat crossed the Pentland Firth to Orkney.

During the reign of James IV, it is stated, a John de Groote of Caithness got a charter to start a ferry to Orkney. According to a writer in the seventeenth century the fare for the crossing was four pounds Scots, which would have had the equivalent in English money of six shillings and eight pence. The Reverend George Barry, writing in 1805, stated that there had been a post office on Swona since 1744, with a boat going to Caithness four times a week. After a road had been built to Thurso in Caithness in 1819, a mail coach arrived and the mail for Orkney was taken to Huna, three miles away, from where a rowing boat crossed the Pentland Firth. In 1828, however, the mail was being conveyed via South Ronaldsay still by rowing boat and then two ferries had to be used between South Ronaldsay and the Orkney mainland. Mail for Stromness was carried by a gig when the road was in a suitable condition. The road between Kirkwall and Stromness followed what is now called the old road, which goes to the south of

Wideford Hill and meets up with the modern road from Kirkwall near Finstown. It is then said to have passed through Stenness a little south of the present road and on to the Bridge of Waithe which then was a causeway one hundred and fifty yards long built of logs on stone pillars. It would have been when the route of the present road came into existence that the Ayre at Kirkwall was bridged and the Bridge of Waithe built. By 1850 coaches were running regularly between Kirkwall and Stromness on an improved road and the farmers, who were becoming wealthy, would have gone to town by gig instead of using a horse and cart. The road that goes from Kirkwall to Stromness via Finstown is the A965, but there is another road, the A964, which skirts Scapa Flow, but it will be a few miles longer. It goes through Orphir, passing Waulkmill Bay where there used to be a Waulkmill, a mill for shrinking cloth, which went out of use during the eighteenth century. It then passes Houton where there is a pier for the ferry to the South Isles and continues on through Clestrain with a good view of the Hoy Hills, the island of Graemsay, Hoy Sound and Stromness across the Bay of Ireland. After passing the mill of Ireland it joins the A965 at the Bridge of Waithe.

In 1856 John Stanger of Stromness obtained a contract to carry the mail from Caithness and he built a wooden ship of about one hundred tons at his shipyard in Stromness. She was fitted with engine and paddles and took over carrying the mail across the Pentland Firth between Stromness and Scrabster, two miles from Thurso, where a pier had been built a few years earlier. In 1874 the railway reached Thurso and the railway company operated a steamship from Scrabster to Orkney and they acquired the mail contract in 1877. In 1882, however, the North of Scotland Shipping Company began to operate the Pentland Firth service using a steamer called the *St Olaf*, which after a few years was replaced with the *St Ola I*. The *St Ola I* must have been a reliable ship for she continued in service for almost sixty years until 1951 when the *St Ola II* replaced her. The *St Ola II* carried motor vehicles but had difficulty in coping with the extra cars in the summer so the company decided to get a drive-on drive-off car ferry, which was built by Hall and Russell of Aberdeen, and it began operating early in 1975 with new terminal and road facilities. Named the *St Ola III*, the ferry was two hundred and thirty feet long, with bow and stern unloading doors, was capable of carrying eighty cars and four hundred passengers, had two independently diesel-driven variable pitch propellers and two bow thrust units to assist in manoeuvring.

Ships on the Pentland Firth crossing to Scrabster have always been based at Stromness and have always had sailing times to suit the arrival and departure of the trains to and from Thurso, while their arrival at and departure from Stromness were the main events of the day and probably still are. The *St Ola I* was sometimes referred to as the mailboat as it carried the mail. Up to the Second World War she called at Scapa to deliver and collect mail, but after the war this was cancelled and she then made the more direct ran past the old Man of Hoy and the highest perpendicular sea cliffs in Great Britain. The Old Man of Hoy once stood on two legs but one was eaten away by the sea. Another sea stack, the Castle of Yesnaby, which still has two legs, can be seen in the sea from cliffs in the West Mainland.

In 1865 George Robertson of Stronsay, a master mariner and a one-time salvage expert, started a steamship service between Kirkwall and some of the North Isles using a wooden screw-driven steamer which was renamed the *Orcadia*. Previous to this, the North Isles had been served by small sailing ships. In 1867 the Orkney Steam Navigation Company came into existence with Mr Robertson as managing director and a new ship, *Orcadia II*, was built for the company to serve the North Isles. After two more steamers had been added to the North Isles service, the *Earl Thorfinn* in 1928 and the *Earl Sigurd* in 1931, the *Orcadia II* was withdrawn, being over sixty years old. During January 1953 the *Earl Thorfinn* was on her way between Stronsay and Sanday when she was caught in a strong gale and she ended up in Aberdeen from where some of the passengers were said to have left the night before.

In about 1960 the Orkney Isles Shipping Company was formed with help from the government. The North Isles ships, besides carrying passengers, also carried livestock, and as the price of coal was increasing the *Earl Thorfinn* and *Earl Sigurd*, being coal-burning ships, were becoming uneconomical to run and the

Orkney Steam Navigation Company didn't have sufficient resources to replace them. The *Earl Thorfinn* was broken up and a new ship, the *Orcadia III*, a motor vessel, was chartered by the new company. The *Earl Sigurd* was kept in use for a while until the *Islander*, another motor vessel, replaced her.

Steamers of the Orkney Steam Navigation Company, had only called at the larger North Isles and the smaller islands had to rely on sailing ships. General Burroughs, who had inherited an estate in Rousay, lived there when he retired from the army and in 1877 he started a steamer service from Rousay to Egilsay, Gairsay, Wyre and the Orkney mainland. The steamer, which was called the *Lizzie Burroughs*, was still running in about 1900 when she was owned by Robert Garden who later used her as a shop-boat. Some island shops were supplied by a boat which would have called at intervals to replenish them with goods.

Shapinsay, the island near Kirkwall, had a steamer service before the turn of the last century. The steamer, the *Iona*, which was built on the island but had her engine fitted south, plied between Shapinsay and Kirkwall for over seventy years carrying cargo and passengers until the *Kyldon* replaced her. These small islands are now included in the timetable of the Orkney Isles Shipping Company as are the South Isles which were previously served by the Hoy Head based at Stromness.

Loganair operate an air service to the North Isles from Kirkwall airport and they also do charter flights and air-ambulance work. The North Isles air service was pioneered by Captain Fresson, a First World War RFC pilot, who in 1933 founded Highland Airways, and started flying regularly between Inverness, Wick and Orkney. He was granted a contract to carry the Royal Mail, and this was the first internal airmail service in Great Britain and Captain Fresson is now honoured by a memorial at Kirkwall airport. About the same time, Allied Airways was established by Mr Gandar-Dower who began a service between Aberdeen, Orkney and Shetland. Twin-engined de Havilland Rapide and Dragon biplanes were used on these routes in these early days of air travel and there weren't the navigational aids that there are today. A plane would have to fly below cloud level when visibility was poor and land on uneven surfaces which would ensure a bumpy landing.

In 1946 Highland and Allied Airways were taken over by British European Airways who started to fly Junkers, a plane that had been used by the Germans as a troop carrier, but they were withdrawn when they proved to be uneconomical and the Dakota took its place. The Dakota was a transport plane used by the Americans during the war which was considered to be very reliable and British European Airways flew them in the north of Scotland under the name of Pionairs. British Airways then flew to Orkney and Shetland in place of British European Airways and then Loganair took over most of the flights.

While writing about transport, I will end by observing that the first motor car arrived in Orkney in 1903 and that by 1905 there was a motor bus service between Kirkwall and Stromness. At the turn of the century most children had to walk miles to school and even in more recent times, before the event of the school bus. Then there was a travelling shop or van, which has disappeared because of high running costs.

In the 1880s, when roads were being improved and coal was plentiful, the earl of Caithness experimented with what was called a steam carriage. It had three wheels and was steered by the front one, while a large tank supplied water to a boiler which fed steam to two small cylinders that produced nine horsepower. The earl and countess once travelled in it from Inverness to Wick and then on to Barrogill Castle near John O'Groats and it is said to have encountered no difficulty even on the high gradients at the Ord, Berriedale and Dunbeath. The carriage carried the driver, a passenger and a stoker, but it only carried coal for a twenty-mile run so must have had coaling stops along the way.

Towards the end of the nineteenth century only part of St Magnus Cathedral, the choir, was in use and many of the windows were blocked up. The choir was divided off from the rest of the church by screens, its walls whitewashed and the floor levelled. Leading members of the community had permission to erect pews there, which were of an assorted variety, and there were galleries and garnished boards bedaubed with colour hanging there. By charter from the king, the cathedral was granted to the burgh of Kirkwall, but in the middle of the nineteenth century the crown claimed possession and the pews and galleries were cleared away. A few years later, however, the town council established its right to it and a pulpit was built, new pews installed and the galleries rebuilt. The cathedral was used for burials up to the middle of the nineteenth century and Earl Robert Stewart and a Bishop Tulloch were buried there. Memorial stones of prominent Orcadians now line the inside walls of the cathedral, and among them is one in memory of a son of James V of Scotland, Lord Adam, who died in Orkney, while another bears the name of the Norse Earl Erlend.

Below the large east window of the cathedral, which is in the choir, lie two memorials. One commemorates John Rae, Arctic explorer who surveyed large tracts of land in northern Canada and made five exploration trips into the Arctic areas, two for the Hudson Bay Company and three in search of the ill-fated Franklin expedition, which had called at Stromness before sailing across the Atlantic. The other memorial commemorates William Balfour Baikie, an African explorer.

Mungo Park, a doctor from Peebles and friend of Walter Scott, offered his services to the African Association to travel inland from the West African coast until he reached the River Niger and then to try to find out where it rose and where it flowed to. After much hardship he returned to the coast having discovered that it flowed to the east. In 1805 he was selected by the government to lead an expedition to the Niger and he followed it eastwards for seven hundred miles, past Timbuktu to Bussa in the country of the Hausa, which is now part of Nigeria. At Bussa, Park and the remaining members of the expedition were either drowned or killed by natives sent by the king of Hausa.

In 1830 the explorer Richard Lander completed Mungo Park's task when he travelled down the Niger by native canoe from Bussa, and discovered that it eventually turned south and flowed into the Gulf of Guinea.

It was now known where the Niger flowed to and it was hoped that a new market for British goods would be opened up so some Liverpool merchants decided to investigate the possibility of trading in that part of West Africa. Liverpool had profited by the slave trade which was now being abolished and ships of the British navy were patrolling the West African coast to try to stop the slave ships leaving. In 1832, at the time when the steamship was being developed, two shallow-draught steamers, specially built for river navigation, entered the Niger delta and steamed up the river. They did some exploration and a little trading before leaving the river, but in the delta eighteen men died. This was attributed to the terrible stench there, but it wasn't from the bad air of the swamps that the disease came, but from the mosquitoes that infested them, for these carried the disease germs which were passed on with their bite. As it was thought that the infection came from the foul-smelling air of the swamps it was given the name malaria, which means bad air. By the time of the Baikie expedition, malaria was being treated with quinine which helps to relieve the fever and there was no loss of life on his ship.

The *Pleiad*, an iron-built screw-driven steamer, under the command of the Orkney-born William Balfour Baikie RN, entered the Niger delta in 1854 and steamed up the main river to its confluence with the Benue, a tributary. The main purpose of this expedition was to explore the Benue and the *Pleiad* steamed several hundreds of miles up this tributary. On the upper reaches, Baikie visited the sultan of Hamaruwa who presented him with a black bull with a small hump. According to Baikie's own written narrative, on his return he lost his way, after his companion had gone back to find out what was holding up the main party. As darkness fell Baikie climbed a tree where he spent the night and smoked half a cigar, the other half of which he kept for his breakfast. In the morning he met some natives and got one of them to guide him to where his ship was. The expedition then proceeded further up the river where they encountered some unfriendly savages who lived in houses which appeared to be surrounded by water. As there was now a danger of the ship going aground they returned to the Niger, and then via the delta to the sea, having spent sixteen weeks on the river. Baikie returned to England and in 1857 went with another expedition to the Niger but his ship, the *Dayspring*, was wrecked on a rock in the river near Rabbi, in the country of Nupe, which was a danger to ships. In 1916, when the railway bridge was built over the Niger at Jebba, which is a bit further upstream, part of the engine of the *Dayspring* was found, and it is now on display at the Jebba railway station. Baikie was stranded at Rabbi for a year before a rescue ship arrived and it was during this long stay that he began to realise that it was possible for Europeans to survive in such a place. From the emir of Nupe he got a grant of land at Lokoja, which is lower down the river and he founded a settlement there. Apart from being a fertile spot, this was a place of great scenic beauty, for here the two wide rivers, the Niger and Benue, met and low tree-covered hills rose up from their banks. Away to the north was the higher ground of the Bauchi plateau, where tin is mined, and where during British rule there was a rest centre for colonial officials. Further north is Kano, a walled town and an important trading centre from where caravans crossed the desert to Morocco. From Lokoja Baikie made what must have been a rather arduous journey to Kano and other northern towns, but a year or so later he died at Sierra Leone on his way home, having been recalled by the government. A steamer from Liverpool had called at Lokoja when the tribes of the delta could be fought off and later a trading company was formed there which became the Royal Niger Company when a British force was stationed there to police the company's territory.

At Calabar in southern Nigeria, a Christian mission was founded as early as 1846 and it was here that the Scottish mission-ary Mary Slessor worked. Some Orcadians may remember the late Harry S Mowatt of Graemsay, who was a Church of Scotland missionary at Calabar and who returned to Orkney in 1950 because of ill health.

In November 1854, the same year that Baikie made his historic voyage up the River Benue in Nigeria, the first edition of the *Orcadian* newspaper was printed by James Anderson and his son. It cost two pence and contained news of the Crimean war. A few years later, in 1859, Washington Irving, the American writer died. His father belonged to Shapinsay and one of his stories, 'Rip Van Winkle', is said to have been based on a traditional Orkney folk tale in which a fiddler returning from a wedding is taken by the mischievous dwarfs known as trows in the islands' mythology into a grassy mound where they were supposed to dwell. Part of the story 'Rip Van Winkle' takes place west of the Hudson River, in the picturesque Catskill mountain region of New York State, where Washington Irving chose to live. He became a celebrity and in 1842 was appointed American ambassador to Spain. When in Europe he visited the writer Walter Scott at Abbotsford in Scotland, but was never at this father's birthplace in Shapinsay. Another well-known American, General Custer, who made his last stand against the Sioux Indians at Little Bighorn in Montana, USA, on 25 June 1876, was also of Orcadian descent, his grand-father being a Cursiter.

At this time the crofters in the Highlands had to exist on a few acres of poor land and the only crop they could grow in any quantity was the potato which was practically destroyed by blight in 1846. Some of the crofters were persuaded by their landowners to emigrate while those who remained voiced complaints about their living conditions. Their grievances were that their rents were too high and they had no security of tenure while they had to work on their landlord's farm at times. In 1881 tenants in the south of Skye asked their landlord for the return of some common hill-grazing land that had been taken from them at the time of the clearances. This was refused so they stopped paying their rents. The sheriff served eviction orders on them, but had to get police assistance from Scotland and five of the rebels were arrested. This failed to stamp out the rising and it spread to other parts of Scotland. In 1884 thousands of crofters in the Highlands joined the rebels in refusing to pay their rents and four candidates supported by the crofters won seats for parliament in the 1885 general election. In 1886 the first Crofters Holdings Act was passed, giving the crofters fairer rents and security from eviction while in 1888 the Napier Commission went to Orkney to see that these changes were being carried out there. With security from eviction and reduced rents, the crofters began to improve their holdings, but ambitious young men still thought that a better living could be had overseas. After a time the landowners became short of money because of the reduced rents they now received from their tenant, so they sold the holdings mainly to the tenants who held them and the tenants then became the owners of the crofts they had improved.

Now that the people who worked the land owned it, new

houses were built to replace the old but and ben type and many of the farmhouses in the islands are said to date from this period. Paraffin lamps replaced the cruisie but peat was still the main fuel used and fresh water still had to be carried from a nearby well. In the towns of Kirkwall and Stromness, however, fresh water was piped from nearby reservoirs but it was only recently that some of the islands had piped water connected to them. Shortly after the last war the North of Scotland Hydroelectric Board was supplying the Orkney mainland with electricity but outlying islands had to wait until recent years to be connected to the network. By the turn of the century the streets of both Kirkwall and Stromness had been paved, if not with gold, with flagstones, and this, combined with grey-stoned buildings, gives them an old-fashioned appearance. Stromness has the atmosphere of a small country town but it is also connected with the sea, having a harbour and houses with private slipways or small beaches big enough for a boat to be dragged up out of the water. The main streets wind through the town and before a new road was built along the shore for the roll-on roll-off car ferries, the bus to Stromness had to use one of these narrow streets where it had to negotiate at least one sharp corner before reaching its terminus near the harbour. Ships of P & O Scottish Ferries make use of Stromness as a berth for the *St Ola* from Scrabster in Caithness and the *St Sunniva* on her way between Aberdeen and Shetland. The islanders gave the name ferry-loupers to visitors from the south, but today this will not always be appropriate for many now go by plane. Previously most would have gone by ferry, hence the name ferry-louper, with the louper probably deriving from loop, i.e. starting and finishing at the ferry.

There is now estimated to be over one hundred thousand acres of arable land in the islands, whereas about one hundred years ago there was only seventy-two thousand acres. The extra land has been reclaimed from heath or hill land where cattle and sheep would have grazed. Because of the cool summers, the grain crops sometimes don't ripen, but with plenty of rain the Orkney climate does favour the growth of grass and the farmer now utilises this more than in the past. The back end of the year is not usually a cold period but it is the wettest, so the cattle are taken inside then to prevent the grazing land being turned into a quagmire with the cattle's hoofs, which ensures a good growth of grass in the new year. In former days the cattle were fed on turnips and hay at this time of the year, and as farms were smaller then the cattle could have been tethered outside at some suitable place on good days. When the tractor took over the haulage jobs on the farm, the horse began to disappear, then as other time- and labour-saving aids were introduced, such as the combine harvester, the tendency has been towards larger farms comprising two or more holdings while the grass is put in a silo for use as winter fodder when the cattle are housed. During the years that followed the First World War, when the price of grain had declined, the farms increased their production of eggs for which a favourable price was then being paid. The grain was fed to the poultry and eggs became a major export from the islands until they became uneconomical. During the 1939 war when there was a large number of government personnel stationed in the islands, dairy farming increased, but after the war there was a surplus of milk being produced. To help the dairy farmers the Milk Marketing Board stepped in and collected the surplus milk from the farms by tankers and the factory outside Kirkwall started to make butter and cheese for export. The rearing of sheep increased but, like the eggs, pig rearing, which had been profitable, became uneconomical, and then beef cattle became the main source of income of the Orkney farmer.

The Reverend George Barry said that sheep in Orkney ran wild on the common land and were small in size. In some places they were allowed to wander on to the shore at low tide, where they ate the seaweed, which made their flesh dark in colour and of a different flavour. On the island of North Ronaldsay, descendants of this old breed of sheep are kept permanently on the foreshore by a stone dyke twelve miles long and six feet high, so that any grass growing in the interior of the island is reserved for the cattle. These sheep on North Ronaldsay live almost entirely on seaweed, and because there was the possibility of oil pollution in the area through the exploitation of North Sea oil, some of the sheep were taken to new breeding grounds by a trust set up to look after the welfare of rare breeds of livestock. Those taken to one of the Channel Islands have multiplied rapidly and as they have access to the shore they go there to feed on the seaweed, so they must have retained a taste for it.

Orkney was represented in the Westminster parliament from the time of the union of England with Scotland in 1707, when an Alexander Douglas became the first member of parliament to represent Orkney. Members of the Douglas family represented Orkney at Westminster until 1768, when a Thomas Dundas took his seat there. The Douglas and Dundas families would have been the most important families in the islands at the time. The allegiance of the Orkney members of parliament varied between the Whigs and Tories, but mainly Whigs interspersed with Tories. In more recent times Orkney continued to send mainly Whigs to Westminster, but under the name of Liberals, which they became known as.

The most well-known Liberal member of parliament was probably Joseph Grimond, who became leader of the Liberal Party. He won his seat in 1950 and held it until he died. During the war he served in the Fife and Forfar Regiment with the rank of major. The Fife and Forfar landed in France in 1944 and with other armoured regiments fought their way out of Normandy against the better armed Panzer divisions of the German army.

I can now say that the next chapter, the last, concerns Scapa Flow, the famous anchorage. The naval base there was known to many service people during the war, who have expressed their opinion of it and the long tedious train journey they had to make from the south, followed by an uncertain sea crossing. While stationed there they described Orkney as bleak and inhospitable which would have referred to the weather. They complained of isolation and boredom, all of which is understandable, I suppose, for it was usually the custom of the forces to take a dim view of most places they were stationed at.

Scapa Flow

On a summer afternoon in 1971 I sat on the slopes of the Orphir hill watching the rabbits darting about in the heather. The water of Scapa Flow shimmered in the sun and towards the east a long stretch of the Caithness coast could be seen projecting past the island of Hoy. A tranquil scene then, but it was not so peaceful during war years when the navy was anchored in Scapa Flow.

It was during the Napoleonic Wars that it was suggested that this stretch of sheltered water would make a suitable anchorage for the navy, but it was never made use of as such until 1914 when war with Germany became imminent. Mr Winston Churchill was First Lord of the Admiralty then and he sent the Grand Fleet to Scapa Flow. It was considered to be a safe anchorage, but it soon became obvious that this was not so when a German U-boat was spotted inside Scapa Flow. Within a year the numerous channels leading into Scapa Flow were blocked with sunken ships, and anti-submarine nets were positioned across the remaining entrances with gates to let ships pass through. The entrance most used by the navy was the one approached from the south either by Switha Sound or the Sound of Hoxa, while the less used entrance was approached from the west by Hoy Sound and the Atlantic. At first there were only naval guns protecting the anchorage, but later gun emplacements were built. The remains of First World War gun emplacements lie in a field overlooking Clestrain Sound, the stretch of water which was used mostly by merchant ships entering or leaving from the Atlantic. A narrower channel between the islands of Graemsay and Hoy was closed with sunken ships.

When the war started, Britain had a larger navy than the Germans and had ships with longer-ranged guns. This should have given them the advantage, but when British ships met the German navy off Jutland, it is stated that the new rangefinders were defective and they steamed within range of the German guns, while their shells when fired passed harmlessly over the German ships. The Battle of Jutland took place on 31 May 1916 and was the largest naval engagement of the war. The Grand Fleet, whose duty was to protect the coast of Britain and her shipping was in the North Sea when a battlecruiser squadron under the command of Admiral Beatty encountered five German battlecruisers and two of Beatty's ships were sunk. A large number of German ships were then seen heading in a northerly direction where the main British fleet was under the command of Admiral Jellicoe, so Beatty broke off his engagement and went to assist. The German fleet was thought to have been in harbour so a large conflict with it was unexpected. Many ships of both sides were sunk after heavy bombardments, and as darkness fell the German fleet returned to harbour, leaving their smaller ships to fight on during the night. Both sides claimed a victory but both sides had suffered heavy losses, and afterwards Germany decided to rely on submarine warfare.

A few days after the Battle of Jutland, Lord Kitchener, the secretary of state for war, arrived at Scapa Flow aboard the destroyer HMS *Oak*, on his way to Petrograd in Russia with a military mission. Early in the war the Russian army had suffered annihilation at the hands of the better equipped Germans. With their railways disorganised and their troops short of munitions, Russian resistance was liable to collapse and the tsarist regime with it, a disaster that the Kitchener mission no doubt hoped to avert. On the afternoon of 5 June, the day that Lord Kitchener and his party arrived, there was a strong gale force wind blowing from the north-east. Kitchener had lunch aboard the flagship *Iron Duke* with Admiral Jellicoe, who suggested a postponement until minesweepers had cleared a channel, but Lord Kitchener was determined not to delay his departure.

The cruiser HMS *Hampshire* had returned undamaged from Jutland, and was now anchored nearby as she was the ship detailed for the trip. She had been built in 1904, and had a speed of over twenty knots, but had insufficient armour-plating by 1916 standards. Lord Kitchener transferred to the *Hampshire* in the ship's pinnace and almost immediately the cruiser got under way, leaving the safety of the anchorage to battle with the tempest outside. Two destroyers had left earlier to search for mines in the water along the route that the *Hampshire* was to take and then joined her later as an escort, but they found it impossible to make sufficient headway in the tremendous seas, so were ordered back to Scapa. By this time the gale was veering to the north-west, a change of wind direction unexpected by Jellicoe and his staff who had re-routed the cruiser from the east, to the leeward side of Mainland, hoping to give it some protection from the storm. Alone, the *Hampshire* now struggled head-on to the raging gale, with the cliffs of West Mainland about two miles to starboard. When just past Marwick Head the cruiser was shaken by an explosion in the fore part of the ship and she swung round towards the shore. A survivor saw Lord Kitchener on the quarter-deck talking to two officers of his staff, but within fifteen minutes, at about 7.30 p.m., the *Hampshire* sank by her bows, rolled over and plunged to the seabed.

A soldier of the Orkney Territorial Army on lookout duty that evening at Birsay saw a ship coming out of the mist, close inshore and suddenly flames and a cloud of smoke burst from behind the bridge, so he immediately reported a ship in distress. After some delay every available ship in Stromness, except the lifeboat, was detailed to go to the help of the stricken ship, while the vice-admiral at Longhope, after asserting that it was the *Hampshire* in distress, ordered four destroyers to sea. They passed the other ships but even so were too late to pick up any survivors alive. One of the lifeboats aboard the *Hampshire* had been launched by hand, because the electric generators had failed, but it was smashed against the cruiser's side by a huge wave spilling the occupants into the swirling water. Some rafts got away and were carried by strong currents and the north-westerly wind towards the Bay of Skaill. One was washed up on to the foreshore of Skaill House, but in the morning those who had managed to struggle up to dry ground were found dead. Other rafts ended up north of the Bay of Skaill in geos, which are narrow openings in the coastline, but as the cliffs here are difficult to scale, few survived. The difficult nature of the coast and the delay in the rescue operations will be the reasons why there were so few survivors, for most of those who did reach land died from exposure on the rocks. Out of the several hundred men the ship carried only twelve survived to tell their tale to the naval authorities.

After a long silence the Admiralty published a paper which claimed that the *Hampshire* had been sunk by a mine. At this period U-boats were laying mines in water around Orkney that the British ships were likely to use, so the mine that sunk the *Hampshire* may not have been laid specially for that purpose. Weeks before the Kitchener mission, news of it had leaked out to a number of countries, a leak which is said to have found its way via Turkish baths in the Strand, London, to foreign agents.

In his autobiography, Prince Yusupov, who was responsible for the killing of the monk Rasputin, stated that he had good reason to believe that the Germans had been informed of the date that Kitchener was to depart through spies at the Russian court. Whatever way the date was leaked, it was known abroad as early as May and would have been of great value to the Germans, for if they could have prevented the visit they would have delayed help for the Russians, so if the *Hampshire* had escaped the mine it would probably have been sunk by a torpedo from a U-boat before reaching Archangel. Secrecy would have had to be essential to ensure the success of such a mission.

Kitchener's death seems to have been surrounded by intrigue and the rescue mismanaged. Irish nationalists were attempting to sabotage British ships at this period and were suspected of plotting to kill Kitchener. Before the war the British government had promised Ireland home rule, but this was postponed when the war started. Sir Roger Casement, a patriotic Irishman, considered that Germany would win, so he decided that Germany was the country to collaborate with. He went to Berlin and got a promise of recognition from the government there for an independent Ireland and also got a consignment of arms for a rising planned in Ireland. Casement landed from a German submarine on the coast of Kerry during May 1916, but was arrested by a police sergeant, and a ship carrying the arms was captured. The rising still took place but didn't have much chance of success and the rebels had to surrender. Their leaders were executed and the Irish National-ists were then suspected of planning to kill Kitchener, probably in revenge. Sir Roger Casement had served in the Consular Service and did valuable exploration work for the government in the Niger delta and the Cameroon areas of West Africa, but it being wartime he was hanged as a traitor.

Kitchener also had enemies in the government who would have liked to have seen him out of the War Office. Lloyd George, who was minister of munitions at the time, failed to supply the tsar with arms that had been promised. He blamed the armament factories, but he was afraid that they may be used against the Allies if Russia signed a separate peace. This was contrary to the policy of the Kitchener mission, which was to prop up a toppling tsarist regime.

A memorial tower now stands on Marwick Head, overlooking the spot where the *Hampshire* sank. A plaque attached to the tower was officially unveiled by a high-ranking officer of the army on 2 June 1926, while HMS *Royal Oak* lying offshore fired her guns in salute, scattering the seabirds on the cliff ledges. It was because of the generosity of Orcadians that the tower was built as the following inscription on the plaque confirms:

THIS TOWER WAS RAISED BY THE PEOPLE OF ORKNEY IN MEMORY OF FIELD MARSHAL EARL KITCHENER OF KHARTOUM ON THAT CORNER OF HIS COUNTRY WHICH HE SERVED SO FAITHFULLY NEAREST TO THE PLACE WHERE HE DIED ON DUTY. HE AND HIS STAFF PERISHED ALONG WITH THE OFFICERS AND NEARLY ALL OF THE MEN OF HMS HAMPSHIRE ON THE 5TH JUNE 1916.

About 11.20 p.m. on 9 July HMS *Vanguard* blew up and sank while at anchor in Scapa Flow in the vicinity of Flotta. The cause of the explosion was said to have been combustion of cordite in the magazine, which would make a layman think of sabotage, but by then strict security would have made this unlikely. After the explosion a huge black cloud enveloped the *Vanguard*, while flying debris fell on other ships at anchor nearby and on Flotta. All through the night the search for survivors went on with the searchlights of the other ships playing on the scene, but out of over seven hundred men there were only two survivors and one of these died from his injuries. The late Lord Mountbatten of

Burma, who was then a young midshipman on board the flagship of the Grand Fleet, was among those who searched for survivors.

When hostilities ceased and an armistice was signed on 11 November 1918, one of the conditions was that the German fleet had to be interned in a neutral port. As they seemed to have had difficulty in getting a neutral country to harbour the fleet, it was eventually decided to take it to Scapa Flow, a decision that the Germans must have accepted although it wasn't strictly in keeping with the armistice terms. The German High Sea Fleet put to sea, led by its battlecruisers, with instructions to rendezvous off May Island in the Firth of Forth at 8 a.m. on 21 November. Two long lines of British ships, with their guns trained on the German fleet, met and escorted it into the Firth of Forth and Admiral Beatty sent a message instructing the Germans to haul down their flags at sunset and not to fly them again without permission. Towards the end of November the surrendered ships were brought to Orkney and moored in Scapa Flow between Lyness and Scapa and this anchorage became their graveyard.

The German ships only had skeleton crews aboard, the rest having been sent back to Germany, and after having spent a bleak winter cooped up aboard rat-infested ships, with poor rations and no shore leave, the German sailors were beginning to get muti- nous and von Reuter, the commander in charge of the German fleet, decided to settle the matter in a rather dramatic way. Germany had not yet accepted the terms of the peace treaty so von Reuter could consider his country to be still at war, which would justify his decision to scuttle his ships. On 21 June 1919, after most of the British ships had left the anchorage on an exercise, von Reuter sent a signal to his ships to scuttle themselves. This action, however, could be said to have done his country a disservice for the German ships would have offset some of the war debts.

On that June day, a party of school children from Stromness were enjoying an outing in Scapa Flow aboard the tug *Flying Kestrel*, one of the ships that had searched for survivors from the *Hampshire*. About noon the German ships near them began to sink and the captain, who had been told to return to Stromness, decided that it would be wiser to tie up his tug to a British ship that was anchored there and they had a grandstand view of the German ships with their flags flying disappearing under the surface of the water. British boarding parties trying to save some of the ships by closing their jammed seacocks managed to beach three destroyers. HMS *Royal Oak*, the ship that was sunk at the beginning of the 1939 war, took aboard sailors from the sinking ships. The battleship *Baden* sank in shallow water, but the rest littered Scapa Flow for years afterwards, some with their super-structures sticking crazily out of the water. The firm of Cox & Dank Ltd obtained an Admiralty contract permitting them to salvage the sunken ships. The destroyers didn't present too great a problem for the salvage men, but the larger ships, after the difficult job of raising them from the seabed, had to be filled with compressed air before being towed to Rosyth for breaking up. Metal Industries, the firm at Rosyth which did this, later took over the salvage work.

The first to make the journey was the battlecruiser *Moltke*, six hundred and ten feet long, which caused some anxious moments for the tugmen towing her. As she entered the Pentland Firth the strong tide took control and carried her and three tugs sixteen miles westwards, but they eventually reached the Firth of Forth after a three-day journey. As she approached the Forth railway bridge, however, the tide again took control and she was swung broadside on to the bridge. The tow ropes were let go of and after passing under the centre span of the bridge the tow ropes were connected up again and they continued on their way to Rosyth.

The battlecruisers *Hindenburg*, *Seydlitz*, *Van der Tann* and others were raised and towed away, while a few that still lie at the bottom of Scapa Flow have provided an attraction for diving enthusiasts who come from all over Europe to view the big ships in their underwater setting.

When war was declared on 3 September 1939, units of the Orkney Territorial Army manned the heavy guns positioned on Stanger Head in Flotta and at Ness west of Stromness. Anti-submarine nets again stretched across the entrances of the anchorage used by shipping, while the narrow channels by which a submarine could have entered were blocked with sunken ships as in the First World War. At least one of these, a rusting wreck of a two-masted sailing ship, had survived from that war but it had been swung out of its original position by the tides, leaving a wider gap than had been intended when it was sunk. This was in Kirk Sound and, while a replacement blockship was on tow somewhere off the coast of Scotland, a German U-boat crept into the Scapa Flow anchorage and sank the battleship *Royal Oak*.

Shortly after the outbreak of war, U-boats were operating around Orkney, gathering information about shipping while German reconnaissance planes flew over Scapa Flow. Photographs taken by these planes were examined by the commander of U-boats in Germany who saw the wide gap in Kirk Sound and thought it worthwhile to send a U-boat to try to get into the anchorage by that channel. At about midnight on 13 October 1939, the U 47 surfaced and entered Holm Sound to be greeted with brilliant displays of the aurora borealis which must have made it more visible from the shore, but would have also helped its captain, Lieutenant Commander Gunther Prien, to navigate past the blockships. He made for the wide gap between the two-masted wreck and another blockship, and with only inches of water between the seabed and the bottom of the U-boat, got safely into Scapa Flow, only to find it almost empty of ships.

A German reconnaissance plane had reported the anchorage as being full of warships but since then they had been dispersed to bases on the mainland of Scotland. The naval authority could have taken warning from the activity of the German planes and sent the fleet to safer bases until the defence of the anchorage was complete. Lieutenant Prien took his U-boat towards the centre of the anchorage but there were no ships there; he then turned about and saw the *Royal Oak* at anchor in Scapa Bay, with another warship, claimed to be the *Repulse*, behind it. The U-boat fired two of its torpedoes at the *Royal Oak* and missed, and one at the ship behind it which probably hit the anchor chain of the *Royal Oak* and exploded. This aroused the men aboard the *Royal Oak* who were recovering from a severe storm they had encountered the previous day near Fair Isle. The U-boat turned and fired a torpedo from its stern tube which also missed. The U-boat reloaded its tubes and turned again towards Scapa Bay and fired another salvo of torpedoes at the *Royal Oak* and had more success this time, for the battleship listed to starboard and sank, taking over eight hundred officers and ratings to a watery grave. Searchlights swept the sky while the U-boat with diesel engines at full speed headed back towards Kirk Sound but there wasn't sufficient depth of water to leave by the same route as it had entered. Lieutenant Prien took the U-boat through the gap between the most southern blockship and Lamb Holm where there was a greater depth of water but where there are difficult currents and it safely reached the deeper water outside. Destroyers had by now detected the U-boat and were dropping depth charges, but it escaped serious damage and returned to Germany where Lieutenant Prien received a hero's welcome and a medal from Hitler. Today a marker buoy sways over the spot where the *Royal Oak* sank, while in St Magnus Cathedral in Kirkwall a memorial plaque commemorates the disaster.

Sir Winston Churchill was then First Lord of the Admiralty and he ordered the eastern narrow channels to be completely sealed with concrete and the barriers which bear his name were built. Many thousands of tons of boulders were dumped as a foundation, on top of which five- and ten-ton concrete blocks were scientifically laid so as to withstand the strong currents. Four barriers were constructed to link the islands of South Ronaldsay, Burray, Lamb and Glim Holms to the Orkney mainland at a cost of over two million pounds and ten lives, and it also serves a peacetime purpose for roads were laid on top. Italian prisoners of war captured in North Africa helped in the construction of the barriers and they also built an unusual chapel on Lamb Holm from old Nissen huts and scrap material, which is open to visitors.

A few days after the sinking of the *Royal Oak*, German bombers flew over the Pentland Firth and dive-bombed the depot ship which was lying off Lyness. They blew a hole in her side below the waterline but salvage men were working in Scapa Flow on the First World War German battleship *Derfflinger* and under their direction the depot ship *Iron Duke* was towed into a nearby bay and beached. One German plane was hit by anti-aircraft fire and the rear gunner parachuted to safety to become the first prisoner of war while the plane with the rest of the crew crashed and burst into flames. At dusk on the evening of 16 March 1940 the *Luftwaffe* again made an attack on the anchorage. Searchlights lit up the sky and anti-aircraft guns sent their shells bursting overhead. Bombs fell at Hatston, Holm, Stenness and one near the cottages at the Bridge of Waithe, killing J Isbister, Britain's first civilian air-raid casualty.

After the defences of the anchorage had been improved, the fleet returned to it and ships of the Allied nations also used the anchorage. Besides the anti-aircraft guns, searchlight units and a balloon barrage to deter enemy planes from flying low were positioned around the anchorage. One anti-aircraft battery was perched on a clifftop at Yesnaby, overlooking the Atlantic, which would have been a windy situation, as would have been an observation post on top of the Black Craig. There was a radio-location station at Netherbutton in Holm for detecting approaching planes and airfields were built, some for the Royal Navy and others for the Royal Air Force. The radio-location station at Netherbutton failed to give a warning of the approaching *Luftwaffe* on 16 March 1940, rather similar to the radar at Pearl Harbor when the Japanese attacked the American fleet there in 1942.

In April 1940 the British battlecruiser *Renown* sighted the German pocket battleships *Scharnhorst* and *Gneisenau* escorting an invasion fleet to Norway. Germany built pocket battleships to conform to specifications laid down at the Treaty of Versailles in 1919, although in 1940 the *Gneisenau* was stated as being equipped with radar that could detect a ship at twelve miles. The *Renown* engaged the *Gneisenau* and damaged her, an engagement that would have marked the beginning of the short Norwegian campaign which started in April 1940 and ended in June of the same year. The German invasion forces landed at their destinations and began to take control of the country. Ships of the Home Fleet sailed from Scapa Flow and Swordfish aircraft from the aircraft carrier *Furious* attacked Narvik and Trondheim with the loss of two planes. The heavy cruiser *Suffolk* bombarded Sola near Stavanger and by the time she arrived back at Scapa Flow she had suffered thirty-three attacks by German bombers. The Allies put small landing parties ashore near Narvik and Trondheim but in June these were evacuated and then the king of Norway was taken into exile.

Whatever the naval personnel thought of their northern base, the sailors would have been glad to return to it after having been tossed about for long spells at sea, but some ships didn't return, such as HMS *Hood*, for example. During May 1941 the German battleship *Bismarck* was reported to have sailed for the Atlantic and warships based at Scapa Flow were ordered to sea to search for her. The *Bismarck* was found in the North Atlantic near the convoy route to America and in the action that followed HMS *Hood* was split in two by the big guns of the *Bismarck* and she sank with her guns firing. Only three of her crew survived. HMS *Prince of Wales* was also hit by *Bismarck*'s big guns but she survived and managed to damage the fuel tanks of the *Bismarck* and the German battleship made for Brest to got repairs done. Winston Churchill gave the order to sink the *Bismarck*, and two days later she was spotted by a Catalina flying boat of Coastal Command west of Ireland and then disabled during an aerial torpedo attack by Swordfish aircraft from HMS *Ark Royal*. The following day, in mountainous seas and poor visibility, she was attacked by ships of the Royal Navy and the *Bismarck* scuttled herself.

In 1942 the *Tirpitz*, a sister ship of the *Bismarck*, lay in a Norwegian fiord surrounded by anti-submarine nets. It had been launched by Hitler himself in 1939 and could now be a menace to the merchant ship convoys going to Russia, which were carrying war material to help Russia in her struggle against the German divisions moving eastwards into the Ukraine. The protection of these convoys was the responsibility of the Home Fleet, but despite this there were heavy losses due to enemy action and also because of the severe weather. The North of Scotland, Orkney and Shetland Steam Navigation Company ship *St Sunniva* was commandeered at the outbreak of the war and while acting as a rescue ship with the northern convoys she turned turtle and sank when her masts and rigging became heavily encrusted with ice. There were no survivors.

After Germany occupied Norway in 1940, many patriotic Norwegians escaped over the North Sea to Britain. They were trained in Scotland so that they could return to Norway as saboteurs. Their escape route was to Shetland and they got there in fishing smacks, a type of boat used around the coast of Norway, so they didn't attract too much attention from the Germans. This boat service between Shetland and Norway was known as the *Shetland Bus*, but there wouldn't have been a regular service and some boats never reached their destination. One boat, captained by a Lief Larsen from Bergen in Norway, left Scalloway in Shetland during October 1942 with two specially designed torpedoes hidden aboard his boat. These were to be guided by trained naval personnel through the anti-submarine nets which surrounded the German battleship *Tirpitz* which was lying in Trondheim Fiord, Norway, but the attempt failed. Captain Larsen, his crew and naval personnel escaped overland via Sweden.

Towards the end of 1943, the pocket battleship *Scharnhorst* was sent to prey on the convoys going to Russia. She was the only large warship the Germans had that was fit to go to sea and she was detected by the radar of the ships of the Home Fleet, lurking in the icy seas off the north coast of Norway. In an engagement she was hit, but being a faster ship she escaped out of the range of the guns of the British ships. As daylight was failing a destroyer of the Royal Navy came across her and was lucky enough to hit her three times with torpedoes and then other British ships in the area came in to finish her off. There were only thirty-six survivors and all the British ships returned to Scapa Flow, although some had been hit by shells from the *Scharnhorst*.

The *Tirpitz* had been moved to Alten Fiord further north when she was attacked by midget submarines which failed to sink her, but the attack left her badly damaged. In April 1944 Barracuda dive-bombers from aircraft carriers based at Scapa Flow attacked the *Tirpitz* in another attempt to sink her but they only damaged the superstructure. Alten Fiord where the *Tirpitz* was still lying was outside the range of our land-based bombers, but there were Russian airfields which they could use. Two squadrons of Lancaster bombers were flown to a Russian airfield where they refuelled and then they flew to Alten Fiord. The Germans heard them approaching and enveloped the *Tirpitz* in a protective smokescreen which hindered the bomb aimers who only made one hit which didn't sink her. The *Tirpitz* was now moved to Tromso which was much nearer to any airfield in Britain. Thirty-six Lancaster bombers had their range increased by fitting different engines and larger fuel tanks, which enabled them to cross the North Sea to Tromso, but the Germans again set up their smokescreen. After the raid a reconnaissance plane radioed that the *Tirpitz* was undamaged. It was now getting late on in the year, but the Lancasters tried again and, for some reason, this time there was no smokescreen and the bombs hit their target and the *Tirpitz* capsized and sank.

In May 1945 ships of the Home Fleet again sailed towards Norway, this time to attack a U-boat depot flotilla north-west of Narvik, and on their way back to Scapa Flow the war with Germany ended. Surrendering U-boats slid into Longhope past the two Martello forts at its entrance and the admiral left Melsetter. The naval base was closed in 1957 but the Orkney Isles Council bought land at Lyness from the Ministry of Defence in 1977 and a war museum was opened there in May 1990. On view to the public is the huge propeller and some of the guns of HMS *Hampshire* which was sunk off Marwick Head in 1916.

Appendix One
The Treaty of Perth, 1266

In 1249, Alexander II of Scotland tried to take possession of the Norse-held Western Isles of Scotland, by force, but he died during the attempt. Some years later, in 1261, his son Alexander III negotiated with Norway for a peaceful settlement and when this failed the Scots invaded the Norse-held island of Skye, where they killed the inhabitants and burnt down their farm buildings. In retaliation King Hakon Hakonson of Norway prepared an invasion fleet and in 1263 sailed for the Western Isles. Henry, the Bishop of Orkney, was one of the envoys sent by King Hakon to try and negotiate a peaceful settlement, but these negotiations had also ended in failure. The Norse who landed on Scottish soil were defeated near Largs, while many of their ships were wrecked by a sudden storm. King Hakon returned to Orkney with what was left of his fleet and he died in the Bishop's Palace there. Alexander III was now in a stronger position and he began negotiations again, this time with Hakon's son, Magnus IV, who persuaded the Norwegian diplomats that the Western Isles were of little value to Norway and they were ceded to Scotland in perpetuum at the Treaty of Perth in 1266. As compensation for the Western Isles, Scotland was to pay the king of Norway and his heirs one hundred merks sterling annually at St Magnus Cathedral in the Orkneys, which then belonged to Norway. Also a sum of four thousand merks was to be paid in instalments of one thousand merks with the first four annual payments. Over the years the annual payments lapsed, probably during the War of Independence, but after Robert Bruce was crowned king of Scotland he kept on friendly terms with Norway by renewing the Treaty of Perth at Inverness on 29 October 1312.

Appendix Two
The Marriage Contract of 1468

Early in the fifteenth century Scotland was in arrears with the payments for the Western Isles again and these together with an additional sum for each default had grown into a considerable amount. Christian I of Denmark, who was also king of Norway, demanded payment, but as negotiations between the two countries produced no results, the matter was submitted to the arbitration of the king of France who was friendly with both countries. King Charles of France suggested a marriage between James III of Scotland and Margaret, the daughter of Christian I of Denmark, as a solution to the problem.

In 1468, a marriage contract was drawn up at Copenhagen in Denmark in the presence of the Scottish ambassadors. In this document, Christian I of Denmark cancelled the Treaty of Perth annual payments for the Western Isles and also the arrears which had accumulated over the years. Christian I was short of money because of wars so, as part of the dowry for his daughter Margaret, he handed over the Orkney Isles as a security for fifty thousand florins of the Rhine until he could raise the money to redeem them. Christian I had promised a dowry of sixty thousand florins, so the Scottish ambassadors were to be given the remaining ten thousand florins before they left Denmark. Christian I couldn't procure ten thousand florins so he threw in the Shetland Isles for eight thousand florins, hoping to find two thousand florins to complete the dowry payment, but this may have never been paid.

The marriage contract also stated that Princess Margaret was to be given the palace of Linlithgow and the castle of Doune in Menteith together with one-third of the royal revenues of Scotland. If James III was to predecease her and she wished to leave Scotland, she would receive one hundred and twenty thousand florins in place of the third part of the royal revenues of

Scotland given to her as a wedding present, less fifty thousand florins, the mortgage price for the Orkneys, which would then become the property of Christian I. This evidently never happened for the Orkneys as well as Shetland are part of the British Isles today. Orkney and Shetland had belonged to Scotland before the Vikings, then Norway took control of them and now, having got their hands on them, Scotland wasn't going to give them up easily. From time to time over the years, kings of Denmark have asked for their return, which Scotland always evaded doing.

A few years after his marriage James III of Scotland relieved Earl William of the Orkney earldom with the king of Denmark's approval and James III became earl of Orkney. At this date the king of Denmark must have still had some say in the affairs of the Orkneys which would have been because they had only been given away as a security. His approval for removing the earl wouldn't have been difficult to get, for Earl William was out of favour with the king of Denmark, mainly because he was rarely in the Orkneys as he had other duties in Scotland. Later, a descendant said, Earl William had lost the earldom because he had helped the duke of Albany, the king's brother and the earl's son-in-law, who was trying to get the throne, so he may have been out of favour with the king of Scotland also.

Appendix Three
Kirkwall's Right to the Cathedral

A charter of Thomas Tulloch, bishop of Orkney, which had the seal of the bishop appended to it at Kirkwall on 15 April 1448, stated that during a General Assembly in the Church of St Magnus the Martyr it was confirmed and in full agreement declared that the right of patronage of the Chapel of St Duthac, situated near Kirkwall, belonged by law and custom solely to the earls of Orkney, their heirs and successors for ever.

This chapel, together with the land of Pickaquoy on which it was sited, was transferred to the burgh of Kirkwall by James III of Scotland in 1486 at the same time that he gifted the cathedral and other lands to the burgh and by the same charter that he granted Kirkwall the status of a royal burgh of Scotland. The chapel had belonged to the earls of Orkney, so it is assumed that the cathedral had belonged to them as well, otherwise the king wouldn't have been able to dispose of it in this way. The king was now earl, having acquired the earldom from Earl William. Kirkwall has been challenged regarding its right to be owner of the cathedral, but never with any success, so it still belongs to the burgh of Kirkwall.

Appendix Four
Some Prominent Orcadians of the Twentieth Century

I will start with J Storer Clouston of Smoogro, Orphir, historian and writer. His most noteworthy book is his *History of Orkney*, an authoritative account of Orkney's past.

Eric Linklater, another well-known Orkney writer, served with the Black Watch Regiment in France during the First World War and later became assistant editor of the *Times of India*. His first novel had the title *White Maa's Saga* and this was followed by many more. One of his early novels, *Magnus Merryman*, has part of the story set in the West Mainland and includes a visit to the Dounby market. It was near Dounby that Eric Linklater spent his youth, in a house near the shore of Loch Harray, which is now the Merkister Hotel.

George Mackay Brown was a poet and writer. He was a native of Stromness, having been born under Brinkie's Brae. He studied at Newbattle Abbey College and Edinburgh University.

Stanley Cursiter, OBE, RSA, was a notable painter of Orkney landscapes who became the Queen's Limner.

Lord Birsay, CBE, QC, MA, LLB, held the position of Lord High Commissioner to the General Assembly of the Church of Scotland in the 1960s.

Edwin Muir, essayist and poet, was born in Deerness, then spent his early years on Wyre before moving south to Scotland and further afield.

Lord Grimond of Firth, a former leader of the Liberal Party and MP for Orkney and Shetland, was born in St Andrews, Scotland. During the Second World War he served with the Fife and Forfar Yeomanry, a Scottish regiment, and later with the 11th Armoured Division. He received a peerage in 1983 and took his seat in the House of Lords.

To end, I will include Peter Maxwell Davies, the English musician and composer. Now a resident in the island of Hoy, he gets inspiration for his music from the land and seascapes of Orkney.

Appendix Five
The Norse Earls of Orkney (except those stated otherwise)

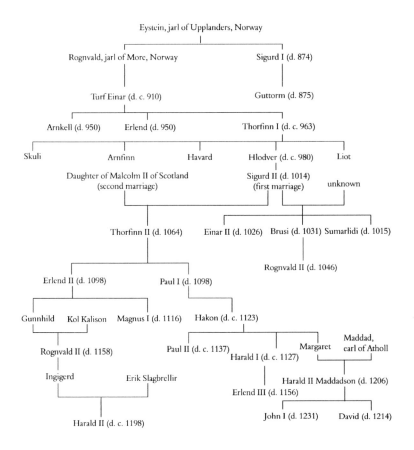

Appendix Six
The Scottish Earls of Orkney

Magnus II, Earl of Angus, Caithness and Orkney (d. 1239) (Magnus II was succeeded in the earldom of Orkney by a Gilbride I, probably a son or brother).

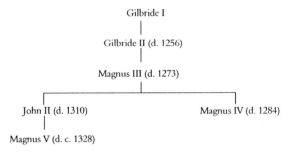

Gilbride I
|
Gilbride II (d. 1256)
|
Magnus III (d. 1273)

John II (d. 1310)   Magnus IV (d. 1284)
|
Magnus V (d. c. 1328)

The Angus Earls of Orkney were succeeded in the earldom of Orkney by an Earl Malise of Strathearn through a marriage connection.

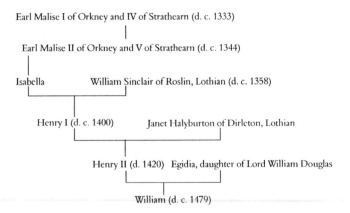

Earl Malise I of Orkney and IV of Strathearn (d. c. 1333)
|
Earl Malise II of Orkney and V of Strathearn (d. c. 1344)

Isabella   William Sinclair of Roslin, Lothian (d. c. 1358)

Henry I (d. c. 1400)   Janet Halyburton of Dirleton, Lothian

Henry II (d. 1420)   Egidia, daughter of Lord William Douglas

William (d. c. 1479)

Earl William was the last hereditary Earl of Orkney and the earldom then became the property of the crown.

Bibliography

Barry, George, *The History of the Orkney Islands*, Edinburgh, 1805 (Reprinted by James Thin, Edinburgh, 1975)

Clouston, J Storer, *A History of Orkney*, Kirkwall, 1932

Clouston, J Storer, *Records of the Earldom of Orkney*, Edinburgh, 1914

Firth, John, *Reminiscences of an Orkney Parish*, Orkney History Society, 1920

Low, George, *A Tour Through the Islands of Orkney and Shetland 1774*, Kirkwall, 1879 (Reprinted by the Melvin Press, Inverness, 1978)

Peterkin, Alexander, *Notes on Orkney and Shetland*, Edinburgh, 1822